Rube Burrow,
Desperado

Rube Burrow, Desperado

Rick Miller

iUniverse LLC
Bloomington

RUBE BURROW, DESPERADO

iUniverse books may be ordered through booksellers or by contacting:

iUniverse LLC
1663 Liberty Drive
Bloomington, IN 47403
www.iuniverse.com
1-800-Authors (1-800-288-4677)

ISBN: 978-1-4917-1781-3 (sc)
ISBN: 978-1-4917-1782-0 (e)

Library of Congress Control Number: 2013922661

Printed in the United States of America.

iUniverse rev. date: 01/31/2014

Table of Contents

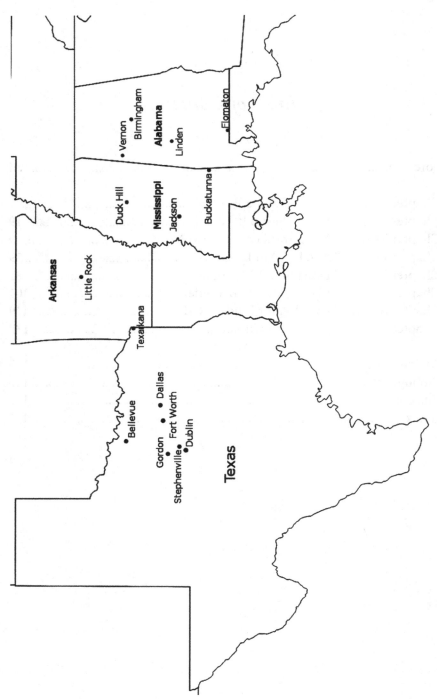

The World of Rube Burrow. Courtesy Janet and Stephen Turner, Hutto, Texas

Foreword

No matter how much tongue-clucking moralization is invoked about the extent of crime, criminals, and violence, there continues to be a widespread morbid fascination with the subject matter. In more modern times, this country experienced the gangster era of the twenties and thirties, with the likes of John Dillinger, Pretty Boy Floyd, and Bonnie and Clyde. Into the forties, fifties, and sixties, America was confronted with another serious crime situation, with various cities victimized and dominated by "families" of the Mafia. From all of this grew a tremendous mythos, as demonstrated by the popularity of such best-selling motion pictures as "Bonnie and Clyde," "The Godfather" (and sequels), "Public Enemies," and so on. From film noir to more extravagant productions, gangster and crime films have garnered top box office proceeds. Today, emphasis on illegal drugs and their obscene profits, provided by foreign cartels and distributed by inner city would-be entrepreneurs, seems to symbolize the dominant crime problem of the current society and our continuing fascination with it.

However, violence in the American Old West has come to be of less and less interest as the oldtimers who were raised on the Saturday western movies at the local bijou pass on, with the possible exception of the Texas Rangers and the overrated "Gunfight at the O.K. Corral." The fictional western productions that inundated the movie and television scene several decades ago no longer compete for public interest, and probably burned out the genre for more decades to come. Aficionados and serious researchers into the events of America's frontier, though, have been ever ready to set the record straight. They have remained fervent in their pursuit of primary sources with which to document and understand the lives and experiences of the good guys and bad guys of yesteryear, correcting the misinformation that for many years has passed as the "history" of this era. This means dealing with the faulty memories found in the memoirs of Old West characters, as well as laziness on the part of some writers who purport to have researched the facts they set forth, when they really just made it up, or relied solely on unreliable secondary sources. Too many so-called "historians" accept secondary sources at face value and repeat incorrect information without any real research or apology. So Billy the Kid continues to kill twenty-one men, one for each year of his life, and Jesse James fatally dispatches eight men with one bullet. All of the old bad men gave money to the widow to pay her landlord, then held up the landlord. None of this is true, but, in the minds of some, why get in the way of a good story?

The popular mental image of the Old West is that of the gunfighter, a la "High Noon," when in reality such folks were quite few, and the era of the Old West gunfighter existed for only a brief period of time. Brief as it was, however, there is more glamour and popular interest that has attached to their adventures, as opposed to the bona fide labors of farmers, ranchers, railroad men, merchants, teachers, etc., who moved west with the growth of the nation. As a result, much of the literature about that period tends to emphasize the stormier, more violent times.

Even in the 1880s and 1890s, there was a reading public anxious to learn about the exploits of the notorious bandits and gunfighters. Badly written pulp paperback books spewed from presses to spread the latest fictional tales of the James-Younger Gang, Sam Bass, Wild Bill Hickok, and a number of lesser names. One of those lesser names was Rube Burrow, an Alabama lad who achieved national fame, albeit brief, for his train robberies and murder. However, unlike Jesse James and Billy the Kid, his fame was shortlived and, except in corners of his home state, he is largely forgotten. This, in spite of the fact that he held up eight trains in four states, as compared to maybe five total robberies by the James-Younger Gang,[1] the three of the Dalton Gang,[2] the perhaps four by Butch Cassidy and the Wild Bunch,[3] and the five committed by Sam Bass.[4] There are only three previously published biographies devoted to Burrow, although he is occasionally mentioned in older anthologies dealing with mail and train robbery. However, the factual errors and omissions in these books call for updated research to provide an accurate accounting.

The first train robbery in the United States has generally been credited to the Reno gang, which occurred near Seymour, Indiana, in October of 1866. However, in January of the same year, Gus Tristram and seven others sneaked aboard an unlocked express car between New York and New Haven, Connecticut, and broke into two safes while the train was en route.[5] For some unknown reason, this theft has not been acknowledged as a bona fide "train robbery" as practiced by the noted outlaw gangs, such as the Reno and James-Younger gangs.

Each gang of train robbers had its unique method of operation. Some obstructed the tracks, forcing the train to stop when signaled. Sam Bass waited until his trains pulled into a station. Others boarded the train as passengers and worked their way to the express car. Rube Burrow forced his way onto the engine, then had the train pulled across a steep trestle where passengers could not get off for fear of falling off the bridge. This cut down on the likelihood of interference while the bandits were conducting their robbing. Unlike the stealthiness of Gus Tristram and his group, a legitimate train robbery apparently required some forceful act directed at railroad or express employees or passengers. There were all types of criminals on the western frontier, ranging from common thieves, safe burglars, and cattle rustlers to stagecoach bandits. The train robber enjoyed a special place at the top of the criminal pecking order. In the public mind, there was a little bit more derring-do involved in overpowering a huge locomotive and its cars, trains then being a symbol of the growth and commerce of the United States. In addition, railroad corporations served as a symbol of the capitalism that led to exploitation of farmers and ranchers forced to cede valuable right-of-way, leading to some popular admiration for the train robbers. But, regardless of the crime involved, the motive of the robbers was the same: greed and easy riches, as opposed to honest toil for an honest day's wage.[6]

Researching these old characters, who seldom left a paper trail, is a daunting challenge, and Rube Burrow is no exception. Considerable disappointment resulted from the lack of courthouse and archival records relating to him and his gang members in Texas, Arkansas, Mississippi, and Alabama. The records of the Pinkerton Detective Agency, now housed in the Library of Congress, were incomplete as to correspondence relating to the chase after Burrow, regretful since they were the first agency employed by the Southern Express Company to attempt tracking down him and his brother. The Southern Express Company, which took the lead in pursuing Burrow, ceased to exist scores of years ago and its records have disappeared. Some correspondence generated in the Post Office Department can be located in the National Archives, and the Regional Archives in Fort Worth yielded valuable information regarding Burrow's Texas crimes and cohorts in court papers stored there.

Considerable reliance in this book is given to newspaper accounts, although this is dangerous ground. Many of the newspapers plagiarized other newspaper accounts, thus perpetuating the mistakes and exaggerations that were often made. The real glue that ties this book together is the book by George W. Agee, *Rube Burrow, King of Outlaws*, a biography released in 1890 within months of Burrow's death. It is amazingly detailed for the time period in which it was written, although that is not too surprising given that Agee, a Southern Express superintendent, played a major role in tracking down the bandit. Even he, though, relied on newspaper accounts that were often incorrect. Two other books about Burrow were published in 1981, but passed on the mistakes and omissions that continue to be repeated, and, further, were not annotated as to sources. For example, one of Burrow's Texas gang has always been identified as Bromley; his name was Brumley. Another gang member named by Agee as Askew was really named Askey. They don't deal in much depth with the gang members who chose to ride the outlaw trail with Rube and Jim Burrow. Hopefully, this book is sufficiently definitive to correct these and other errors and finally set the record straight.

In writing this and other books about Old West characters, villains or otherwise, I have been confronted by academicians, some of whom have never written a book, who insist that research such as this is not complete until the protagonist has been psychoanalyzed: Why did Rube Burrow turn to crime? Why did he pick on trains as his target? My honest response is: How the hell would I know? Noted historian Robert M. Utley, relying on the works of Richard Maxwell Brown, wrote that there are three groups of contributors to "outlaw historiography": popularizers, long on drama and short on fact; grassroots historians, or avid, detailed archivists of fact; and, third, professional historians, "masters of patterns and trends and context and analysis and interpretation."[7] I happily confess to being in the second category, and this book has been diligently researched to present an accurate, factual record, ample fodder, I suppose, for those "professional historians" who would attempt speculation or "educated guesses" as to what made Burrow and the others in his life's story tick. Plain and simple, speculation and guessing are not history. I leave it to the reader to make up his or her own mind as to "why" Rube and Jim Burrow and the others did what they did. In the meantime, "what" they did is amply explained correctly, and if the evidence is there that legitimately supports historical speculation, great.

I am greatly appreciative of the generous contributions made by a number of folks in Lamar County, Alabama. Among them, Barbara Woolbright Carruth of Sulligent spent years collecting information about the bandit and his family. Valuable photographs were provided by Floyd Mack Morris, Jr., Sulligent, and Clanton Dubose, Vernon.

For information buried in the National Archives and Library of Congress in Washington, D.C., grateful thanks go to professional researchers Rebecca Livingston (Silver Springs, MD) and Cypress Communications (Alexandria, VA). Also, important documentation was received from the following: Donaly Brice, Texas State Library and Archives (Austin, TX); National Archives, Southeast Region (Morrow, GA); Rodney Krajca, Archivist, National Archives, Southwest Region (Fort Worth, TX); Archives, Ohio Historical Society (Columbus, OH); Dr. Dawn Youngblood, Tarrant County Archivist (Fort Worth, TX); Mississippi Department of Archives and History (Jackson, MS); Arkansas Historical Commission (Little Rock, AR); Circuit Court Clerk (Texarkana, Miller County, AR); Circuit Court Clerk (Linden, Marengo County, AL); County Clerk (Vernon, Lamar County, AL); Linden *Democrat-Reporter* (Linden, AL); Meredith McLemore, Archivist, Alabama Department of Archives and History (Montgomery, AL); Tarrant County District Clerk (Fort Worth, TX); Mary Jane Harbison, Library Technical Services, Amon Carter Museum of American Art (Fort Worth, TX); and Green Lawn Cemetery (Columbus, OH).

Chapter One

"... As Good a Boy ..."

*Allen Burrow, patriarch of the Burrow family. Courtesy
Floyd Mack Morris, Jr., Sulligen, Alabama*

Reuben Houston Burrow, purportedly at age fifteen.
Alabama Department of Archives and History.

The four Burrow brothers: back row, l. to r., James Burrow and John Thomas Burrow; front row, l. to r., William Jasper Burrow and Reuben Burrow. Courtesy Floyd Mack Morris. Jr., Sulligent, Alabama.

Virginia Burrow, Rube's first wife. Courtesy Floyd
Mack Morris, Jr., Sulligent, Alabama

The train slowly chugged to a stop at the depot in Birmingham, a large crowd expectantly waiting in the chilly pre-dawn hours. City policemen, stationed to keep order, restrained the crowd on the platform as a knot of men backed a wagon to the baggage car. Gingerly, a plain pine coffin was lifted from the train onto the wagon, then hurried into the express office before the morbidly curious crowd could interfere. Hundreds of persons surged against the windows of the express office, peering intently through the glass.

An official of the Southern Express Company, assessing the throng of people, decided to open the coffin and allow the spectators to file into the office for a brief glimpse of its contents. With the lid removed, the corpse of Rube Burrow was revealed, clothed in a blue homespun shirt, blue jeans pants, and a faded coat, all of which were filthy and had seen much better days. Several hundred persons slowly passed by the coffin to catch a last glimpse of this vaunted desperado, the body's unseeing gray eyes half open, with a two-month growth of beard and matted, dirty hair.

Once the crowd had thinned, it was decided to allow a photographer to set up his equipment to memorialize the capture and death of the outlaw. The coffin was leaned upright against the corner of the office, and later against the railroad car, and for effect the body was posed with the outlaw's weapons in his hands, his large black cowboy hat added to complete the scene.[8] With a flash of light the image was captured to establish that the once elusive bandit had finally been caught.

Who was this Rube Burrow? Newspapers dubbed him "Red Rube" in an effort to popularize a bloody image as a deadly bandit, and one New York newspaper even dubbed him the "King of Outlaws," whose soiled legacy was on a par with that of the infamous Jesse James and other noted Old West desperadoes. Burrow's trail of crime had crossed five state lines, from Texas to Florida, and resulted in an extended manhunt by scores of committed detectives and lawmen, all of whom had been repeatedly frustrated by Burrow's almost miraculous ability to escape their clutches. One of the supervising detectives involved in the pursuit penned a biography within months of Burrow's death, also labeling him the "King of Outlaws." Although largely forgotten today except among Old West aficionados, Burrow's deeds once captured the imagination of the nation's press, and he was even championed in pulp potboiler novels of the 1890s. Since that time, though, only a few attempts have been made to accurately trace his life and criminal career, achieving varying degrees of success. He, too, like so many other Old West bad men through the years, morphed into a sort of Robin Hood, an attribution that is totally removed from reality.

*   *   *

Not unlike many of the notorious characters of frontier times, Rube Burrow's early life is not well documented, and only sparse information and anecdotal accounts have survived. His father, Allen Henry Burrow, was born on May 21, 1825, in Maury County in south central Tennessee. The following year his parents migrated to Franklin County, Alabama, settling in 1828 in what ultimately became Lamar County, a mountainous region dotted by oak and pine forests located on the Tombigbee River in a remote northwestern part of the state on its border with Mississippi. Considered a poor county at the time, with a population of 12,142 in 1880, it consisted primarily of small-scale farmers raising corn, potatoes, and livestock, as well as cotton, goods that were shipped to markets at Mobile and New Orleans. Late in the nineteenth century, lumber mills began harvesting the timber in the area, and tanneries went into production.[9] In August of 1849, Allen Burrow married a local girl, Martha Caroline Terry, 19, and the two began a family on their small farm.[10] Martha Burrow, it was later claimed, was adept at the ancient art of "curing," and had "occult powers of curing cancers, warts, tumors and kindred ailments, by the art of sorcery."[11] Some descendants of the Burrow family, however, disagree with that description. Instead, it is insisted that Martha Burrow was a licensed midwife with a strongly religious gift of healing who kept a bountiful table for her large family and guests who might drop by.[12]

The children quickly followed. In 1888, Allen Burrow stated he had eight living children, two others having died.[13] John Thomas Burrow, the eldest, was born in 1849, the same year as his parents' reported August marriage, hinting the couple may have been compelled to formalize their relationship sooner than later.[14] The second child, about 1850, was Jasper, later reported to be "slow," another claim disputed many years later by some descendants of the family, but who was described by his father some thirty-odd years after Jasper's birth as "an invalid" and "almost constantly in my care."[15] The next eldest child was William Joseph, born about 1854, then a daughter, Sarah Francis, came along about 1855. Reuben Houston Burrow, the fifth child, was reportedly born on December 11, 1855, although the birth year has often mistakenly been written as 1854.[16] Rube's younger brother, James Buchanan Burrow, was born in 1858, followed by Mary Susan in 1860, Lucinda in 1862, Martha Keziah about 1866, and Anna Eliza in 1868.[17]

According to Rube's first biographer, George Agee, Allen Burrow worked hard to support his burgeoning family. Agee reported that the elder Burrow, although himself possessing a very limited education, briefly taught school in Lamar County in addition to working his small farm. This came to an abrupt end when parents withdrew their children from the country school because the teacher insisted that his students spell "every monosyllable ending with a consonant by adding an extra one, as d-o-g-g, dog; b-u-g-g, bug."[18] The primary income for the family came from the farm over which Allen Burrow toiled, near the Fellowship community about three miles from Vernon, the county seat of Lamar County.[19]

The Burrow family's peaceful existence was interrupted by the Civil War in 1861 when the patriarch and other members of the family served with an Alabama cavalry regiment. After the war, Allen Burrow returned to farming, but also reportedly engaged in illegal moonshining, not an unusual calling then in that remote part of Alabama. According to Agee, Allen Burrow was indicted about 1876 for illicit distilling, leading him to disappear for several years. Some sort of compromise was subsequently arranged with the authorities and he reportedly returned to his farm and family.[20]

Rube Burrow's boyhood, by all credible accounts, was an average one for a country boy in that time. While his later letters reflect a poor grasp of spelling and punctuation, he nevertheless had a minimal education. Agee described Burrow's early life as uneventful.

> He was known as an active, sprightly boy, apt in all athletic pursuits, a swift runner, an ardent huntsman and a natural woodsman. He possessed a fearless spirit, was of a merry and humorous turn, a characteristic of the Burrow family, but he

developed none of those traits which might have foreshadowed
the unenviable fame acquired in after-life.[21]

This description was subsequently taken to task by period newspapers after Rube Burrow achieved notoriety, the contradiction stemming from an effort through sensationalism to increase circulation by emphasizing the lurid rather than the facts. The press preferred to tell of a young boy with a strong predilection for outlawry, the result often approaching absurdity. One account of Burrow's early life was that the young boy had sufficient education to develop a fondness for the pulp dime novels so prevalent then, especially a book relating the exaggerated exploits of Jesse James and his gang. Accordingly, Rube was supposed to have set his sights on becoming a road agent. Armed with a single-barrel shotgun given to him by his father and wearing a crude bag with eyeholes over his head, a 15-year-old Rube Burrow allegedly waylaid a neighbor on the road from town and took his money. The neighbor, however, knew the boy and told Allen Burrow what happened. According to the tale, the old man was supposed to have thrashed his son soundly and made him return his ill-gotten loot.[22]

Another account promulgated by the *New Orleans Time-Picayune* claimed that when Burrow was nineteen years old (although he was already in Texas), he killed a companion in Alabama when an argument ensued during a hunting trip, but for which he was not prosecuted.[23] Even yet another account had a young Burrow organizing a "band of thieves" that made illicit whiskey, with him even trying counterfeiting on his own without success.[24]

The ultimate of silliness on this subject was published in 1889 by the New York *Daily Tribune*. In that article, Rube was supposed to have repeatedly crept away from the play of his schoolmates to climb over a nearby hill where passing trains occupied his attention, "following the express-car with a loving gaze as long as it was in sight." The article also claimed that when the teacher asked her students to bring in a problem for the others to solve, Rube presented: "If A is in an express-car with $30,000, and B drops in with a shotgun, at the end of five minutes how much more money will B have than A?" His teacher was supposed to have tearfully lamented that they were not aware at the time that "B" was a cipher for Burrow.[25]

Whether any of these stories were true or not, and there is no official record of them, Allen Burrow never corroborated them. He was, instead, quoted as tearfully praising his son: "Rube was as good a boy as any man ever raised." He "was a good worker. He plowed and split rails and gave me as little trouble as any boy I ever raised. He never disobeyed a command in his life. He went to school at times. We have always been poor people, and I couldn't send him all the time, but he learned how to read and write and was tolerable at figures."[26] He asserted that Rube was "a smart lad without a lazy bone in his body."[27] In all probability, Rube Burrow experienced the average life of a frontier lad, becoming familiar with and thriving in normal outdoor pursuits as well as working on the farm with his family, without any foreshadowing of his future criminal career.

At some point, however, life in Lamar County apparently palled on young Rube Burrow, perhaps even due to the lure of glamorous fables about cowboy life in the West, and he decided it was time to leave the family home. Such migration to the "wild west" was not uncommon during this period, many a family leaving behind the designation, "G.T.T.," indicating that they had gone to Texas. One account puts the year of Rube's departure as 1872 and another in 1874.[28] The target of his journey was the Texas home of an uncle, Joel A. Burrow, a Confederate veteran like his younger brother, Allen, who had left his farm in Lamar County and moved his wife, Martha, and at least five children in the early 1870s to Wise County in north central Texas. In January of 1874 Joel Burrow purchased 160 acres on the west fork of the Trinity River, near the town of Aurora, where he established his farm, followed by another eighty adjoining acres in 1883.[29]

Exactly how and when young Rube Burrow arrived in Texas, where he lived, and what he did is not documented. His first biographer, George Agee, wrote that he "worked awhile on his uncle's farm, but soon drifted into that nondescript character known as a Texas cowboy," transgressing the law "only to the extent of herding unbranded cattle and marking them as his own."[30] There is no record that Burrow ran afoul of the authorities for any crime prior to 1886. At some point, Burrow met young Virginia Catherine "Cata" Alverson of Tarrant County, born about 1853 as the tenth child of Henderson B. Alverson.[31] The two reportedly married in 1875 or 1876, although the exact date and location is unknown, Wise County being one possibility and

Tarrant County the other.[32] It is very likely that the acquisition of a bride acted as somewhat of a civilizing influence on the young Burrow, if he needed one, and he earnestly pursued farming and livestock activities to support his new family. On March 6, 1877, a son, William Thomas, was born. The 1880 Wise County census shows his family living near Uncle Joel, and also lists a one-year-old male, Allen, likely named after Rube's father, but the child does not appear after that and likely died.[33] A daughter, Mary Florence, was born on March 18, 1881,[34] and it is possible that Cata had complications giving birth, as she reportedly died in 1881.[35]

The Pinkerton Detective Agency later asserted that Rube was a member of the Masonic Order, and at some point was supposed to have worked for the Mexican Central Railroad, although when and where has not been documented.[36] Rube's younger brother, Jim, also likely lured by a desire for adventure, joined him in Texas several years after Rube had arrived, perhaps about 1876. Their father briefly visited his brother Joel in Texas, also visiting with his sons, apparently satisfied with the efforts the young men were making to establish themselves.[37]

However, one anecdote passed down that, if true, reflects the two maybe were not totally averse to an occasional departure from the mundane routines of domestic life. According to the tale, a waterhole located in Erath County, Texas, about five miles northwest of the small town of Alexander, was homesteaded around 1860 by a man named Charlie Papworth and his wife Jenny, where they subsequently had two children. While Charlie was gone on a trip, Jenny and one of her children disappeared, later suspected of being murdered and allegedly dumped in a nearby well by a neighbor named Brownlow. Fearful of Papworth's revenge, according to the tale, Brownlow misled a group of vigilantes into trying to lynch Papworth as a cattle thief, but the unfortunate victim was able to escape and fled the country. Thereafter, the abandoned Papworth house was believed haunted by Jenny and her baby, and a number of people reported seeing their specters.

Rube and Jim were said to have been frequenting a local saloon in Alexander and heard the tale of the ghost. According to the tale, the bartender bet them $200 they could not stay in the Papworth house for three days and nights, and the boys readily took him up on it. As the story goes, they were supposed to have seen the ghostly two the first night, but looked away. On the second night, the ghosts supposedly floated through a wall toward them and they opened up with their pistols, running for their lives when their ammunition was exhausted.[38] As with other anecdotes, there is no corroboration of this tale.

Jim reportedly had his own brush with the law in nearby Fort Worth in Tarrant County. Although the year is unknown, former Tarrant County Judge C.C. Cummings, in 1888, recalled that a young Jim Burrow came before him years before charged with stabbing a man in the northwestern part of the county. His trial was memorable because Jim's lawyer made the mistake of doubting the prosecution's version of how the assault occurred, and invited the burly state's witness to demonstrate on him. Needless to say, the witness pounded heartily on the hapless lawyer, and the jury was sufficiently convinced to return a verdict of guilty. It was for naught, though, as the defendant had taken "leg bail" and disappeared from the courthouse, according to Judge Cummings.[39] However, there is no official record that Jim Burrow was ever arrested in Tarrant County, so perhaps the good judge was basking in the limelight of the revelation of the Burrows as train robbers in order to tell a good story.[40]

A fully grown Rube Burrow stood about six feet high, maybe an inch or more taller, and weighed a slender 160 pounds. With light, sandy hair, a broad face with a full forehead, he often affected a thin moustache. Perhaps because of a break at some point in his life, his left arm was a little shorter than his right. On occasion he reportedly used an ointment known as "Hair Vigor" to darken his hair. He reportedly drank alcohol, but not to excess, and did not use tobacco in any form. Not much of a gambler, only occasionally playing a card game called "seven-up," he was gregarious and fond of telling stories during informal gatherings with friends, and was noted as a good horseman as well as a marksman.[41] Another anecdote passed down glamorized Rube as the only cowboy in Erath County, Texas, who could rope and tie a particularly roguish steer.[42]

According to Agee, the two brothers remained together in Texas until 1880, when Jim returned to Alabama, perhaps accompanying his father.[43] Back in Lamar County, Jim moved in with his sister Mary and her husband, William Berryhill, helping his brother-in-law with his farm.[44] On November 21 of 1880, he married local girl Martha Elizabeth Hankins, 16, and the couple had two children by 1885.[45] In 1884 Jim bought 442 acres in Lamar County in order to establish his own farm.[46] However, Jim and his family, perhaps at the behest of brother Rube, moved to Erath County in west central Texas, where Rube was now residing. It was reported that after his wife's death in 1881, Rube took his children back to the family homestead in Lamar County, staying for a few months, then returning alone to Texas.[47]

The 1886 Erath County tax assessment rolls show that Rube Burrow paid $2.50 on two horses or mules, but owned no property. Peculiarly, there was also listed in the county a Reuben D. Burrow, who likewise owned no property.[48] This second Rube Burrow, who has been confused with Reuben H., was a saloonkeeper in Stephenville, the county seat, and was frequently in trouble with the law for liquor violations.[49] While newspaper accounts at the time of Rube's death claimed that he bought a farm, no deed records have been located reflecting any purchase of land in his own name.

The thirty-one-year-old widower Rube courted and wed Adeline A. Hoover, 26, in Erath County on December 30, 1886.[50] The daughter of farmer James Abraham Hoover and Nancy Elvira Underwood Hoover, Adeline was born on November 29, 1860, one of ten children.[51] In the 1870s the Hoover family had lived in Benton County, Arkansas, and by 1880 was living in Johnson County, Texas.[52] However, what the bride likely did not know on her wedding day was that her new husband had already inaugurated his criminal career. This marriage was later described as an "unhappy" one that soon resulted in separation.[53]

After the death of his first wife, Rube had gathered about him various associates, ostensibly as employees of his and Jim's stock business, all of whom would become involved in his criminal pursuits. One of those was 42-year-old Henderson Brumley. Born Marion Henderson Brumley in McNary County, Tennessee, on December 2, 1844, to James C. and Melinda Brumley, he came with his family to Texas at an early age, settling first in Titus County. During the Civil War, he served as a private in Company H of Colonel James E. McCord's Frontier Regiment of the Texas Cavalry along the Red River, primarily to head off raiding Indians.[54] By the time of the 1870 census, Henderson was working his farm in Erath County, now married and with a six-month-old daughter.[55] In the early 1870s, because of ongoing raids by Indians, he served as a Texas Ranger minute man along with his brothers, Calvin and William.[56] Ultimately his family blossomed to ten children, and in the 1880s he was working as a cattle drover.[57]

During the time he lived in Erath County, Brumley became friends with the younger Rube Burrow.

Another associate was Napoleon Bonapart Thornton, known to his friends as "Nep." Born January 8, 1847, in Bienville, Louisiana, to Isaac and Tabbitha Thornton, Nep Thornton was living with his older brother, David, in Erath County in 1860. By 1870, he was working his own farm, married to Nancy A. Alverson since August 1869, with a one-month-old child. Mrs. Thornton was an older sister of Virginia Burrow, Rube's first wife, thus making Rube and Nep brothers-in-law. Thornton had at one time worked with another brother-in-law, W.H. Ledbetter, at Ledbetter's salt works in Shackelford County, on one occasion in the early 1870s killing an Indian attempting to kidnap a child and helping to chase off another party of Indians.[58] Nep and his wife ultimately had four children.[59] In 1874 he purchased 127 acres in Erath County, although he sold them in 1883.[60] He, too, joined Brumley and Jim and Rube Burrow, the four coming to a decision to take the outlaw trail.

What urge came over these four men to forsake the honorable vocations they had been pursuing as farmers and stockmen is unknown, perhaps the glamor derived from pulp novels about Jesse James and other desperadoes. Perhaps there was an economic motive stemming from an inability to satisfactorily support their respective families, such as a severe drought occurring in 1886. It's possible that fantasies of quick riches through criminal means overwhelmed the harsh realities of the hardscrabble life of a rancher or farmer. Whoever came up with the idea and convinced the others is also a mystery. Nevertheless, the decision was made and off they rode to implement a newly-hatched criminal career.

It is not formally documented, but the early press claimed that the four men ventured north into the Indian Territory, now Oklahoma, about November of 1886 to rob an Indian woman supposedly in possession of some wealth. The mission failed for some reason, one newspaper claiming that she vigorously fought them off.[61] Thwarted in their first foray into crime, the four began the return ride to Texas, and soon fixed on the idea of train robbery.

In the nineteenth century, railroads were a dominant part of the nation's economy, being a primary transporter of goods and passengers. They represented an important cog in the livelihood of farmers, ranchers, and industrialists, and were critical to the growth of the nation, both economically and geographically. Some, though, resented the railroad corporations for the often ruthless manner in which right-of-way for the steel rails was obtained, often by eminent domain procedures forced through at the local courthouse. So when bandits saw railroad express and mail cars as a quick way to get wealthy, albeit at gunpoint, not everyone was critical, but, instead, silently applauded the criminal acts. The first railroad holdup in the United States is generally credited to the October 6, 1866, holdup near Seymour, Indiana, by the Reno gang.[62] The glamor of daring outlawry generated by reports of such robberies was accelerated by the larger-than-life efforts of the James-Younger gang, and Sam Bass in 1878, making such robberies seem to would-be outlaws much easier in execution than the toils required to rustle cattle, as well as safer than attempting a bank holdup amidst the presence of alert law enforcement and an armed citizenry. It is thus easier to understand the decision of Rube Burrow and his three cohorts to decide on train robbery, in the fashion of the James boys, as a new mode of getting rich quick.

Bellevue was a small watering station for the Fort Worth and Denver Railroad, sitting south of the Red River in Clay County some seventeen miles southeast of the county seat, Henrietta, and approximately eighty miles from Fort Worth, just west of the Montague County line. The southbound train slowed and stopped shortly after 11:30 a.m., on Saturday, December 11, 1886, to take on water at the tank about a half mile north of the small village. Three men were seen riding up to a small house on the north side of the track at the tank, tying their horses to a fence, then walking around and sitting in front of the house.

The three men, unmasked and dressed in a manner normally associated with cowboys, walked leisurely toward the engine, then suddenly produced revolvers and ordered Engineer Claude Ayers and his fireman to hold up their hands. The bandits removed gold and silver watches and a small amount of cash from the two men, as well as from the train's porter and baggagemaster. The four trainmen were then ordered to stand in line away from the train, guarded by one of the bandits.

The other two robbers proceeded to go through the two passenger cars, bypassing the mail and express cars, although one newspaper account later stated that no mail or express car was attached to the train.[63] One of them, the apparent leader, was described as slightly over six feet tall, spare built with a wiry figure, light brown hair, sandy moustache and goatee, and wearing a reddish brown wool skull cap. The second bandit was described as "a man of less intelligence," of "brutal looking countenance," who stood five foot eight inches, had dark hair and eyes, a black moustache, and a week's growth of beard, and who wore black pants, a gray brown coat, and coarse boots, appearing to be thirty-six or thirty-eight years of age. The robber guarding the trainmen was a "pronounced blond with light sandy hair, red moustache, and blue eyes, wearing a white hat.

One by one, passengers were forced to disgorge their valuables, then instructed to move to the forward passenger car. Initially the two robbers individually searched each male passenger, then, apparently growing impatient, merely requested their victims to hand over their cash and valuables. When the passengers first became aware of what was happening, they feverishly scrambled to hide what valuables they could, such as drummer Howard Peak, who hid his cash under a coal shovel on the coal box. It was later calculated that some $12,000 in cash and valuables were overlooked by the bandits. When the robbers commenced their search, one lady indignantly asked aloud: "Is there not a man in this coach with bravery enough to raise a finger?" Someone to the rear of the car, his hands in the air, responded, "Yes, ma'am! Every man in this car is brave enough to raise all his fingers!" Another passenger, Tom Wagoner, had $400 on him and an expensive pin given to him by his wife. He turned to a young lady sitting next to him and asked her to hide them for him. When she asked how, he blushed and managed to sheepishly stammer, "Ex-excuse me, miss, but put them in your stock-stocking." He ended up turning over only twenty-five cents to the bandits.

Army Sergeant Charles Conner and three soldiers of Company F, 24th Infantry, all African-American, were in the smoking car guarding two soldiers headed for prison. Conner prepared his men to fight off the robbers, but was approached by passengers to desist, concerned that innocent persons would be caught in the crossfire, also speculating that the possibility of additional robbers outside the train would make resistance futile. As a result, the soldiers' arms were meekly surrendered to the three train robbers, an act that would later create a public uproar and accusations of cowardice.[64] On arrival at Fort Worth, the soldiers went quietly to the city marshal's office to borrow some pistols for the remainder of their trip.[65]

Once the robbers had gone through the passengers, they walked leisurely back to their horses and slowly rode off. It is unknown where the fourth man of the bandit group was during the robbery, perhaps remaining with the horses. The amount of their take was variously estimated at from $100 to $200 in cash, plus some watches and pistols. It was evident that this was an amateur holdup; the robbers had overlooked the express and mail cars, if there were any, and risked possible gunfire from armed passengers. Fort Worth and Denver Railroad Superintendent C.L. Frost was notified of the holdup by telegraph from Bellvue and immediately transmitted a $600 reward offer, $200 for each robber. Several posses left Fort Worth to search for the fugitives.[66] Telegrams also were sent to former Texas Ranger Lee Hall, then in the Indian Territory, and Ranger Captain Sam McMurray at Quanah, Texas.[67] McMurray and five men, at Frost's request, made a search for the robbers until December 18th, but returned to camp empty-handed.[68] McMurray wrote Texas Adjutant General W.H. King that he believed the robbers were the "Brooking outfit" from Baylor County, who had broken out of jail at Seymour, Texas, sometime before.[69]

Reporting the holdup, the *Fort Worth Daily Gazette* opined prophetically: "If the Bellevue train robbers are not caught the chances are that there will be another train robbery within sixty days."[70] Perhaps the editors had in mind the memory of Sam Bass and his gang, who in the early spring of 1878 held up four trains around nearby Dallas in less than fifty days. It was even speculated that one of the robbers in the Bellevue robbery was no less than Frank Jackson, Bass's trusty lieutenant who survived the gang's bloody shootout in Round Rock, Texas, in July 1878, and who had immediately disappeared.[71] For a week or so after the Bellevue robbery, lawmen scoured the countryside in all directions for any suspects, here and there stopping strangers who had the unfortunate luck of being in the wrong place at the wrong time, but subsequently released as not being the culprits sought. One man who was arrested and subsequently indicted, Dick Shephard, was later released in January after a hearing before the United States Commissioner in Wichita Falls when he was able to establish an alibi for his whereabouts and the trainmen were unable to positively identify him as one of the robbers.[72]

Whether or not the Bellevue robbery had been planned, or Rube and his associates merely happened on the stopped train while returning from the Indian nation and decided to take advantage of the opportunity on the spur of the moment is unknown. But the amateur robbers had gotten away, albeit with a little cash, but perhaps it was this minor success that whetted their appetite for more.

Chapter Two

"I Can't Stand It!"

William Brock. William A. Pinkerton, Train Robbers and the "Hold Up" Men. Jamestown, Va.: William A. Pinkerton, 1907.

U.S. Marshal William L. Cabell. Texas Collection, Baylor University.

Deputy U.S. Marshal Ben E. Cabell. Texas Collection, Baylor University.

As the excitement of the Bellevue robbery subsided and lawmen gave up their efforts to locate them, the robbers must have taken stock of their paltry gains. Clearly, the real money was to be found in express and mail cars, not among the passengers, and the four bandits were ready to try again. The men must have prepared ready excuses to give their wives in order to account for their absences from home and family.

The next target was closer to home. They selected the tiny town of Gordon, settled among several small hills in southern Palo Pinto County, just north of its border with Erath County. The village had been designated as such by the Texas and Pacific Railroad in 1874, and served as the primary loading place for coal for the railroad from the nearby community of Coalville.[73] Just who was involved in the planned robbery with Rube is unknown. More than likely, he was assisted by his brother Jim, as well as Henderson Brumley and Nep Thornton. However, George Agee wrote that they were also accompanied by Harrison "Askew." Subsequent court documents establish that it was actually a Harrison Askey who was associated with the gang, although his exact role in the robbery is not documented anywhere except in Agee's account. The likely candidate is James Harrison Askey, who in 1880 lived in Callahan County, three counties to the west of Erath County. Born April 18, 1843, he served in the 22nd Texas Confederate Cavalry during the Civil War, and married Sarah T. Williams in Hunt County, Texas, in 1866. He and his wife farmed while their family grew.[74] How and why the almost 45-year-old man became associated with the schemes of Rube Burrow is unknown.[75]

At 2:28 a.m., on Sunday, January 23, 1887, just forty-three days after the Bellevue robbery, the eastbound Texas and Pacific train slowed as it briefly stopped at the Gordon depot, then began to pull out for the chute about 200 yards past the station in order to refuel with coal. As the train lumbered along, Engineer John Berquist and Fireman Jake Weeman were surprised when two men clambered aboard the engine with them. Berquist asked them what they were doing, and started to stop the train to put them off. The two intruders produced sixshooters and told them to keep moving if they wanted to live. The train chugged past the coal chute without stopping, and as it approached the high trestle over Barton's Creek about a mile or so east of town, the train's headlight peered through the pitch dark blackness and illuminated a pile of rocks stacked on the track. Ordered by the robbers to stop, the train was brought to a halt with the engine, tender, baggage, and express cars completely across the bridge where the rocks prevented further movement. The passenger coaches, sleeper, and mail car behind them were astraddle of the trestle, making it next to impossible for passengers to get off the train without falling into the creek bottom.

Additional men came out of the darkness, and the two trainmen were ordered to the ground at gunpoint, the bandits careful to keep the two men between them and possible gunfire from the passenger cars.[76] Agee writes:

> At the point where the train was stopped, Jim Burrow, Thornton, and Harrison Askew [sic], a recruit who had but recently joined the robber band, were in waiting. As the train pulled up, Askew's nerve failed him, and he cried out, "For Heaven's sake, boys, let me out of this; I can't stand it." Askew's powers of locomotion, however, had not forsaken him, and he made precipitate flight from the scene of the robbery.[77]

There is no mention of this episode in contemporary accounts of the robbery, which included firsthand interviews with witnesses as to what occurred. That Askey was involved with the gang in some manner, however, was corroborated by subsequent court documentation. The trainmen were all of the impression that the robber band was composed of a total of six to eight men. The actual number of robbers is unknown, and the excitement and adrenalin generated by the assault on the train likely led to exaggerations in how many bandits were there. Most probably there was a total of five, if Askey was present.

The two robbers who mounted the cab accompanied the engineer and fireman back to the express car and yelled at the Pacific Express agents inside to open the side doors, there being no end doors. The request was refused and the robbers opened up a fusillade at the car. One bandit threatened, "If the damned dog don't open it, we'll burn the car and roast him alive. We've got to have that money!" When one bullet narrowly missed the head of Express Agent A.W. Lesky and lodged in a water cooler behind him, he quickly relented and opened the door. Two of the robbers clambered aboard and gathered up the money packages after using the agent's key to unlock the safe, the take totaling an initial estimate of about $10,000. This amount was later downgraded by express officials to $1,850.[78] Lesky later described the unmasked leader of the gang as being tall and thin, weighing about 165 pounds, with light hair and eyes, a month-old beard and a longer moustache. He wore a cap and carried two Colt .45 revolvers. The other robbers, who were masked, had the appearance of cowboys, with spurs on their boots and all wearing white hats. When one of the train men bravely asked why one robber, the apparent leader of the gang, was not wearing a mask, another of the men told him, "You see, the captain don't live around here, and he is not in danger of being recognized."[79]

When the train halted, Conductor Tom Brennan hurried forward through the cars to find out the reason for the delay. However, when he heard the shots fired, he wheeled about and returned to the passenger cars, ordered the lights turned out, and advised the startled passengers to hide their valuables. As with the Bellevue robbery, a frantic scramble began to secrete cash and jewelry.[80]

In the attached mail car, H.M. Price, the postal clerk on duty, and clerks Richard Griffin and W.S. Tipton, who had been sleeping, realized that a robbery was in progress and began hiding as many registered packages as they could, concealing a large number among loose mail sacks and other hiding places. Only nine packages were left in sight. Once the robbers were finished with the express car, they had the engineer pull the train a little further ahead so that the mail car would clear the trestle. The postal clerks had only one pistol, a .38-caliber Smith & Wesson with two bullets in it, so on the command to "open up," they readily unlocked the door. "Boys, you might as well give up; I have been in two or three affairs of this kind, and while I never killed anybody, I'll be Goddamned if I am afraid to do it," threatened the gang leader.[81]

When Rube, unmasked, held out his hand for clerk Griffin to pull him into the car, Price bristled and disgustedly asked, "See here; don't you think it is a little tough to have to pull a man into your car to rob it?" The robber replied, "That's all right; help me in." Even though the robbers were reminded that this was the United States mail, the brigands searched the car and quickly located thirty-four registered packages.[82]

In the smoking car when the train was stopped was William Henry Lewis, the sheriff of Dallas County who was returning a prisoner to Dallas. When Lewis heard the shots, he realized what was happening and asked four African-American soldiers in the car if they had any guns. When they replied affirmatively, he told them to come with him to resist the robbers. Only one, a sergeant, accompanied him, and the sheriff stepped out on the steps of the car over the trestle and called out in the darkness, asking if any trainmen were ahead. A robber responded, "Damn you, be quiet." Lewis then opened fire with his pistol while the soldier suddenly ran back into the car saying, "They're not bothering the federal papers nohow," later saying that some of the passengers made him mad by calling them "militia." Lewis fired only two shots, and the robbers returned the fire. When the trainmen being guarded by the robbers yelled at him that he might shoot one of them, Lewis retreated back into the car with the other passengers.[83]

The robbers briefly considered robbing the passengers, but figuring that there had been more than sufficient time for cash and valuables to be frantically hidden, decided to leave with what they had. In addition it would have been too difficult to enter the passenger cars, poised as they were above the creek bottom, at least without again moving the train. The train robbers then quickly disappeared into the darkness, leaving the trainmen to remove the rocks from the track and resume their journey to Fort Worth, where it arrived two hours late.

The train moved on to Dallas and, since the federal crime of theft of the mails was now involved, United States Marshal William L. Cabell directed his son, Deputy U.S. Marshal Ben Cabell, to take a special train to Gordon and begin a hunt for the robbers. "I expect to have a big crowd at Gordon and to make it hot for the robbers," declared the marshal confidently.[84] By one o'clock that afternoon, the special train was whistling through Fort Worth on its way to Palo Pinto County, a posse aboard with bloodhounds ready to give chase.[85] As with the Bellevue robbery, lawmen scoured the countryside in all directions looking for and stopping possible suspects.

One of those stopped on January 25 about twelve miles from Gordon was John Augustus Houston, a nondescript-looking young man. Agent Price identified him as one of the men who held him at gunpoint, although he quickly added that he could not be positive.[86] Houston, who worked on his father's farm in Erath

County, emphatically denied that he was involved in the robbery, but was nevertheless locked up in the Dallas County jail based on his identification by trainmen as perhaps one of the robbers.[87] On the 26th, Deputy U.S. Marshal S.P. Maddox arrested Robert Settle at Cisco in Eastland County, Settle's home being about eight miles from Gordon. Maddox was "not certain whether he has the right man or not," but because he was carrying $210 he deemed the man somewhat suspicious and took him into custody.[88] Marshal Cabell received word of three additional arrests and averred: "God bless them. I will capture them all or drive them out of the country!"[89] These three men, John Oxford, Sam Beall, and Ike Clark, were arrested at Gordon and brought to Dallas.[90]

During the investigation at Gordon, buggy wheel tracks were spotted within several hundred yards of the trestle where the Gordon robbery occurred. On the day before the robbery, a hack, accompanied by two horsemen, had been seen going toward Gordon, and seen again on the morning of the robbery. The vehicle was tracked to Oxford's farmhouse thirty-seven miles from Gordon where he, Beall, and Clark were arrested. Settle was also believed to have ridden with the buggy. This evidence was later disputed by members of Oxford's family who made their own investigation.[91] A postal inspector examining the robbery scene found the remains of a fire where it was apparent that the robbers had divided the loot and burned express papers. Marshal Cabell stated, "The captain of the gang is still at large, and is an ubiquitous curse, but I have three squads on his trail, and I think that his capture is certain." From their jail cell in Dallas, the five men adamantly denied being the robbers.[92]

On Thursday, February 10, a preliminary examination of the men in custody in Dallas was held before U.S. Commissioner John Burford. The hearing continued for over a week through Friday the 18th, at which time Commissioner Burford discharged Ike Clark and Sam Beall for lack of evidence, and set a $2,500 bond each for Settle, Oxford, and Houston, in spite of extensive alibi evidence presented on their behalf. Another suspected train robber, John Cole, also was released on a $2,000 bond.[93] Houston, who had come down with pneumonia and was unable to post bond, remained in jail until he could finally raise bail on April 18.[94] On March 17, Houston, Settle, Oxford, and a man named Sam Ravenscraft were indicted for the Gordon robbery by a federal grand jury at the federal court in Graham, Young County, as well as for putting the life of Postal Clerk Griffin in jeopardy.[95]

In the meantime, the Burrow brothers and their criminal associates returned to their routine lives and respective homes in Erath County. Probably with the help of his share of the loot, on February 15 Jim Burrow purchased 100 acres in Erath County from a widow, Mrs. Sarah E. Brock.[96] Agee wrote that the two brothers bought a few head of stock and resumed an honest living, at least for a while.[97] Sometime in January or February, 1887, shortly after the Gordon robbery, the brothers invited an acquaintance, William L. Brock, to come work for them on their stock farm, which he did. It is unknown if Brock was related to the widow that sold Jim the farmland, but could be a possible explanation for how Brock came to their attention.

William Lawrence Brock, born on April 23, 1856, in Franklin County, Georgia, to James M. and Jane Brock, lived in Brazos County, Texas, by 1870.[98] Coming from San Antonio, by 1885 he was living in Erath County, where, on May 27 of that year, he married Elisabeth Victoria Acker, 17, the daughter of Erath County farmer Joseph Benn Acker and Martha Jones Acker.[99] Brock had known Rube and Henderson Brumley for about three years, and Jim Burrow for about a year.[100] Not a property owner, he was assessed in 1886 for taxes on four cows and five hogs.[101] Agee described Brock as wholly illiterate, unable to read or write.[102]

On March 10, 1887, Rube wrote two letters, one to his father and another to his brother, John Thomas, in Lamar County, Alabama. Rube reported that Jim's wife, Elizabeth, had given birth on February 28 to their third child, a son, and that both were doing well. He wrote that they were intending to plant corn. Apparently he sent them fifty dollars, asking that his father keep twenty and that John keep thirty. For some reason, suggesting that things were already wrong with the three-month marriage to his young bride, Adeline, or that they had already separated, Rube asked his mother "too pick mee out one of the prityest widows in ala. I will come home this fawl." He also wanted his father to use some of the money to buy a gold ring for his younger sister, Anna Eliza.[103]

However, perhaps running low on cash, Rube began considering another robbery. Brock had been working for the brothers on their farm, when Rube commented that "there was no use of a man being poor if he just had a little nerve." If two or three men had enough nerve, he observed, they could hold up a train "and rob it anywhere in the world . . . just as easy as robbing a hen's nest." He then asked Brock if he thought he had enough nerve to hold up a train, finally revealing that he and Jim had pulled off the robbery at Gordon.[104] But Brock remained noncommittal for the time being, at the same time giving no reason for the Burrow brothers to mistrust him.

In May, Rube and Jim decided they could hold up a train themselves, and planned on trying Gordon again. However, they were not in time to catch the train when the two arrived.[105] Returning south to Erath County, the brothers again recruited Henderson Brumley, leaving Brock behind, and set northward to rob the train at Benbrook, outside Fort Worth in Tarrant County. But strong spring rains poured down on them and they were unable to cross a flooded Brazos River without using a public ferry and risking being later identified. Returning to Erath County some six to eight days later, the trio told Brock about raiding a "bee gum" within a mile and a half of the Benbrook station and carting it away some 200 to 300 yards to make off with some very rich honey. They gave Brock a saddle that they had obtained somehow during the trip.[106]

On Wednesday, May 18, another gang, with a more brutal method of operation, headed by Brack Cornett and Bill Whitley, robbed the International and Great Northern train at a station fifteen miles from Austin, Texas, not far from the grave of train robber Sam Bass at Round Rock. A passenger was shot in the hand when he rested his arm in an open window, ultimately resulting in amputation, and a brakeman was wounded.[107] There was no indication, though, that lawmen at the time thought the separate robberies were connected with those committed in North Texas by the still unidentified Burrow brothers.

After another eight to ten days of working with Brock on the farm, Brumley, who lived about nine miles from the Burrow place, rode over to the farm and proposed that Brock accompany them to Tarrant County for another try at the Benbrook train. Brock finally agreed, and the four immediately set about gathering up horses for the journey. Brock did not have a horse, and the Burrows had none "that they wanted to ride." They knew there would be some hard riding and did not want to ride their own stock. Brock knew of two horses belonging to a man named Able, who lived near Brock's father-in-law. Rube knew of two other horses near the Burrow farm, a roan mare belonging to a widow named Ann E. Greer, who lived in the next household to the widow Brock, and the other, a sorrel belonging to a man named J.L. Standifer.[108] Waiting until dark, Rube and Brock went to Green's Creek, which ran east of the village of Dublin, near Able's farm, and located the two horses hobbled on the prairie, one of them a "flea-bitten" grey horse. They took them back to the Burrow farm and kept them out of sight, hobbled in nearby timber. The next evening, again after dark, the two Burrows, Brock, and Brumley got the other two horses, and, at about eight or nine o'clock, they started their trek to Benbrook in Tarrant County.[109] Nep Thornton did not go along because he had to tend to a sick child.

Riding all that night and the next day, they arrived within three miles of the Benbrook station in the evening.[110] Located a few miles southwest of Fort Worth in Tarrant County and settled as early as the 1840s, Benbrook became a station for the Texas and Pacific Railroad in 1880 and, as a community grew around it, the town adopted the name.[111] The four men camped the rest of the night near a small creek, sneaking over to where the Burrows had previously stolen the honey, and took more. The men stayed in their camp all the next day awaiting their opportunity and playing "Seven-Up" to determine who would board the engine. At about 6:00 in the afternoon of Saturday, June 4, 1887, leaving their horses at the camp, Jim Burrow and Brock, who lost two out of three "Seven-Up" games, walked to the station. Rube and Brumley headed on foot toward the bridge over Mary's Creek, eight miles southwest of Fort Worth, where they planned to stop the train. At the station, Jim and Brock met two men and asked how soon the train was due, then went and sat on the platform, Brock whittling a stick, and occasionally the two paced while they awaited the arrival of the train.[112]

At about 7:45 p.m., as the sun was setting, the eastbound Texas and Pacific train from El Paso pulled into the Benbrook station. As the train was ready to pull out and resume its journey toward Fort Worth, Jim Burrow and Bill Brock, who had blackened their faces with burnt cork and were wearing red handkerchiefs over the lower part of their faces, jumped aboard the engine. Pistols were presented to the engineer, John Baker, and fireman, and the trainmen were ordered to get the train moving, stopping when it got to the bridge over Mary's Creek. As the engine approached the bridge, Rube Burrow and Brumley, standing on the track, waved the train to a halt, the passenger cars straddling the bridge just as at Gordon, and cross ties stacked across the rails ahead of the train. Brumley was wearing an imitation fur cap and Rube also a cap, although neither wore a mask over their blackened faces. The trainmen were ordered out of the engine cab, and, while they were guarded by one man, the other three knocked on the express car and demanded that the door be opened.

When the train stopped, a passenger, A.C. Wilmeth, a surveyor from Scurry County, was standing on the outside platform of a passenger car talking with the train's brakeman. The two stepped to the ground and walked forward towards the bridge where they saw some men standing. Someone told them to get back on the train, but they kept walking. After a second order, Wilmeth stepped up on the platform but kept looking. "Keep your head back, God damn you!" and a gunshot from Jim Burrow punctuated the darkness, leading the surveyor to quickly reenter the car. Both he and the conductor told the other passengers that the train was being robbed. As before, a mad scramble ensued to hide cash and valuables. The passengers could see the four robbers, but also, off to one side some fifty feet, they saw a man mounted on a gray horse who rode off just before the train started up again, and it was assumed that he was the captain of the marauders.

At the express car, Rube gave his hand to the express agent to help him aboard the car. Rube did not have a pistol and, when Jim asked him if he wanted it, he said he did not. "I can lick these fellows with my fist." Rube gathered what money he could in the express car, about $1,350, putting it in a seamless grain sack. While rummaging through the car, he found a gold watch in a paper sack. He asked the messenger to whom it belonged. When the messenger claimed it, Rube handed it over to him, telling him that he did not want it or anything else that belonged to him; he just wanted the express money, not some individual's property.

Rube jumped down from the express car and the bandits headed toward the mail car, the second car behind the tender, which was not yet off the bridge. The engineer was ordered to pull the train up to clear the mail car. When the bandits demanded entry to the mail car, Richard Griffin, the same postal agent who had been on the mail car during the Gordon robbery, remarked to the other postal agent, R.T. Skiles, that the voice giving the order sounded exactly like that at Gordon. Griffin immediately opened the car door, telling the men with pistols pointed that he had nothing with which to hurt them. As at Gordon, he again had to help Rube aboard, then showed him the table where the mail was located. Skeptical on finding only three registered packages, Rube searched the car, once more handing over another gold watch he found hidden in a paper sack that belonged to the other mail clerk, Skiles. "I don't take anything that belongs to a working man." Later, Skiles could only comment about the robbery that "this thing is growing fearfully monotonous."[113]

Calling out "Adios" to the mail agent, who responded in kind, Rube jumped to the ground from the mail car, and the four bandits, after telling the engineer to get his train moving, backed away over a nearby wire fence. Engineer Baker brazenly asked Rube if the outlaws could spare a cigar, and Rube asked Brock if he had one in his pocket. Disgusted at this informality, Brock snarled, "The devil with a cigar." Crossing the fence, the four men watched as the train gathered steam and resumed its journey to Fort Worth, its relieved passengers cheering uproariously that they had not been touched.[114] When the train had put some distance between them and the bridge, someone aboard the train fired two or three shots back at the robbers, which the four men ignored. They began walking up the creek bottom for a short way, then stopped and pulled their boots off, walking barefooted in the creek to kill their scent in the event that bloodhounds were used in the pursuit, and then continued walking about a mile and a half across a prairie and farms. At some point before reaching their camp and horses, they put their boots back on.

They rode out immediately, ferrying themselves across the Brazos River before daylight with a stolen boat, and stopping the next day about four or five miles from Bluffdale, on Berry's Creek just west of the Erath County line with Hood County. They divided the money equally, burning the registered packages in which the money had been contained. The four then rode on to Stephenville, first stopping for a short time at the home of A.F. Harris near Bluffdale, northeast of Stephenville, where a number of people were gathered and where the bandits ate dinner before riding on. Within two or three miles of Stephenville, they stopped and laid down until darkness fell. The robbers then rode home, skirting the town, and, after Brumley left them to return to his home, the Burrow brothers and Brock arrived at the Burrow farm about nine that evening.[115]

In the meantime, as soon as the train reached Fort Worth Saturday evening, Tarrant County Sheriff Ben H. Shipp and eight men departed for Benbrook aboard a special train with horses and three bloodhounds that were kept at the county jail. A larger posse under Fort Worth City Marshal Sam Farmer left a little later on horseback, headed north to possibly cut off the bandits, who were thought to have perhaps headed in that direction. However, despite high hopes of a quick capture, the sheriff and six of his posse wearily returned about dawn Sunday morning, their horses jaded and their faces stamped with regret at not overtaking their prey. The bloodhounds had eagerly struck the bandits' trail for some distance until water thwarted the scent where the robbers had waded Mary's Creek. The posse discovered that the man on the grey horse at the robbery was W.P. Murphy, a Benbrook constable who had seen the stopped train but did not suspect that it was a robbery.[116] A disappointed Sheriff Shipp said, "I'd have given a clean $100 out of my own pocket to have caught 'em, but we did our best." In neighboring Parker County, Sheriff Henry S. Sisk mounted a posse to also search for the bandits, but also to no avail.[117]

United States Marshal William Cabell also ordered a posse of five deputies into the field, instructing them to "use all diligence in overtaking them." The Texas and Pacific Railway Company announced a $500 reward for each of the train robbers.[118] In Austin, Governor L.S. "Sul" Ross ordered Texas Ranger Company F under Captain William Scott to move from East Texas to Weatherford in Parker County in order to assist in the search. They arrived there on June 13, encountering some criticism from local citizens who took exception to the idea that their community was a "resort for outlaws and train robbers." It was apparently for this criticism that the Rangers shortly thereafter removed their camp to Cisco in Eastland County, just west of Erath County.[119] Captain Sam McMurray of Company B pursued a suspect named A.T. Barnes to Austin, but let him go when he could not be identified.[120]

In the meantime, the fact of three unsolved train robberies was beginning to wear a little thin with the public, and questions were asked about when the robbers would be caught. The *Fort Worth Daily*

Gazette even printed a sarcastic poem penned by a local wag in which the train robbers hooted at the authorities, one of the stanzas of which averred:

> We have heard about the Governor of the Lone Star state,
> And the reward he offered in hope to seal our fate;
> It is best we keep quiet, and therefore write this letter—
> We will see your 500, Governor, and go you 500 better.[121]

To compound the sarcasm, the Cornett-Whitley gang held up another train on June 18 east of Flatonia in Fayette County southwest of LaGrange, near the Fayette-Gonzales County border. This time, they clubbed the express agent and split his ears with a pocket knife when he refused to give them the key to the safe.[122] This outrage led Wells, Fargo & Company to offer a $9,750 reward for the capture of the Flatonia robbers.[123] Cornett would be shot to death in February of 1888.[124] Given this outbreak of train robberies, Marshal Cabell wrote United States Attorney General Augustus Hill Garland pledging "I will leave no stone unturned—leave nothing undone in my district" to nab the robbers and to protect mail trains. It was his opinion that he was after "a well organized band of robbers that extends from the Canadian River in Indian Territory to the extreme southern limits of the state." However, he asked for more funds to meet the expenses incurred by him and his deputies in attempting to track them down, asserting that he had been compelled to spend more than three times as great as the fees that he had collected.[125] He and his fellow United States Marshals in Texas, John Rankin and R.B. Reagan, also asked the Attorney General to allow them to work together in tracking down the robbers.[126]

A flurry of concern about the spate of robberies in Texas now began to assert itself. The Merchants and Manufacturers Bureau of Fort Worth sent a resolution to Governor Ross on June 20, offering its hearty support to the governor "in any energetic and extraordinary measure he may think proper to adopt for the prompt suppression of train robberies, and punishment of the guilty."[127] Others saw an opportunity to get involved. Private Detective Thomas O. Bailes, a former deputy sheriff and constable in Bell County, Texas, wrote Texas Adjutant General W.H. King offering his services to either capture the robbers or "run them out of the state," if the state would pay his expenses and he received all rewards when the job was done.[128]

On July 4, representatives of the Texas Traffic Association, whose membership was composed of the various railroads and express companies in Texas, met with Governor Ross in Austin. The governor proposed to commission up to 390 railroad employees as special Rangers, to be attached to companies of the Frontier Battalion, but to be under the control of and armed by the railroads and assigned in proportion to the number of employees in each railroad company.[129] After considerable discussion among the railroad companies, some of who favored sponsoring these "train rangers" and others who did not, the idea died.[130]

The outbreak of train robberies in Texas led to increased alertness. This paid off on July 6 in Bell County, in Central Texas, when a station operator at Pendleton spotted several suspicious men around the depot and alerted the train dispatcher at Temple. The dispatcher armed four or five men and had them board the northbound passenger train. When the would-be robbers signaled the train to stop, the guards opened fire and the bandits fled for their horses in a nearby thicket.[131]

As before, lawmen were scouring the countryside for the train robbers, stopping and arresting anyone who even came close to the descriptions given by the trainmen. On August 13, U.S. James Warren was arrested in Palo Pinto County by a special deputy marshal. Two brothers, James S., 28, and Ben F. Hughes, 26, were arrested in Potter County in the Panhandle, and Harvey Carter, was also arrested in Palo Pinto County on September 7.[132] The U.S. District Attorney for the Northern District of Texas, Charles B. Pearre,[133] was convinced of the guilt of the two Hughes brothers and of Carter. Mail clerks Tipton, Griffin, and Price viewed and identified them at the Dallas jail. Other witnesses claimed that the Hughes boys had bragged of robbing the train at Gordon and others claimed to have seen them at Gordon at the time of the robbery. While the evidence was not as strong against them in regard to the Benbrook robbery, Pearre was nevertheless convinced that the right men were in custody.[134] After an examining trial in federal court in mid-September, the bail for the Hughes brothers was subsequently set by the U.S. Commissioner at $2,500 each, and $3,000 for Carter. After a second examining trial for the Benbrook robbery, the Hughes brothers, as well as Carter, were quickly indicted on three federal charges stemming from the robberies.[135]

Oblivious to the ongoing efforts to nab them, the Burrow gang struck again, this time choosing to strike once more at Benbrook three and a half months later. Again, on the evening of Tuesday, September 20, 1887, as Engineer John Baker was pulling out of the Benbrook station bound for Fort Worth, two men wearing handkerchiefs across their lower faces jumped into his cab from opposite sides and, with pistols leveled at his head, ordered him to take the train to the bridge over Mary's Creek. When Engineer Baker asked the men where they wanted him to stop, "At the same place you did before" was the response. The train was stopped as before with the passenger cars astraddle the bridge. The engineer casually asked one of the bandits how much they got in the first robbery. The reply was: "we had nothing to do with that affair." When reminded that he had just ordered the engineer to stop at the "same place," the robber just laughed.

The two trainmen were ordered to the ground and marched to the express car where three additional robbers, also masked, appeared and demand was made for the express agent to open the door. The Pacific Express messenger remained silent and the brigands opened fire at the door and battered it with a coal pick. With the door about ready to yield to the violence, the messenger realized that continued resistance would be futile and opened it. Three of the robbers leaped in and ransacked everything in the car, including tearing the grates out of the stove, emptying the contents of the safe into a bag. It is unknown for sure who all of the five robbers were, but it may be fairly assumed that, in addition to the Burrow brothers, they were Henderson Brumley, Nep Thornton, and Bill Brock.

When the shots rang out, the passengers once again engaged in the frantic ritual of scrambling to hide their valuables. One of the passengers, J.L. Glenn, a Hood County deputy sheriff, drew his pistol and, along with another passenger with a small five-shot pistol, stood ready to do combat if their car was invaded.

The outlaws left the express car and headed for the mail car, where perennial victim Richard Griffin, the mail clerk, and another clerk, S.A. Stewart, waited. Allowed admittance to the car, one robber quickly searched it and all registered packages were removed. The five then quickly melted away into the darkness of the timber skirting the creek and disappeared.[136]

When the train later pulled into Fort Worth and the news of the robbery was broadcast, Sheriff Shipp and Marshal Farmer once more mustered a posse, and they, their horses, and bloodhounds were transported by special train to Benbrook. But the bandits had a good head start and the posse returned to Fort Worth on Wednesday after losing the trail at a camp meeting place where multiple tracks obliterated any clues. The bloodhounds were unable to detect a traceable scent.[137']

The train robberies now stopped being a novelty. "The train robbing business has become too common for it to form a very interesting subject of conversation," commented the *Fort Worth Daily Gazette*.[138] The newspaper editorialized: "There is but one way to stop train robbery in Texas, and that is to kill somebody whenever the attempt is made."[139] Across the area, lawmen were again stopping possible suspects. On September 21 in Parker County, Sheriff Sisk arrested John Shadle, a Palo Pinto County farmer, who reportedly resembled one of the bandits, and took him to Dallas.[140] The admonition of the *Gazette* bore fruition on October 14 when an express messenger on the Southern Pacific Railway shot and killed two robbers in far West Texas when the train was stopped between El Paso and Ysleta.[141]

By now, the criminal cases against some of those arrested had moved toward trial. John Houston was acquitted of the Gordon robbery in federal court at Graham on October 31 after a four-day trial.[142] On November 4, 1887, after an eight-day trial, a federal jury at Graham took only minutes to acquit John Oxford, Robert Settle, and Sam Ravenscraft of the Gordon robbery, followed by Harvey Carter's acquittal on November 12. Almost ninety witnesses had testified in all of the trials.[143] But another jury there convicted the Hughes brothers for the Gordon robbery on November 12, a consequence likely of their idle boasting about being involved, and they were sentenced to life imprisonment at hard labor.[144]

In mid-November, after renting out their farm, Rube and Jim traveled back to Lamar County, Alabama, for a visit with their family. Agee writes that Rube took his two children with him, although not his wife, from whom he was likely now separated. It is possible that the children were already in Alabama with the brothers' family.[145] Rube and Jim spent several weeks there, not looking over their shoulders for lawmen, greeting friends and neighbors who had no idea what the men had been up to. They had pulled off four successful train robberies, and the authorities still had no idea who they were looking for. Innocent men had been sent to prison for their crimes, but that was not their worry.

Chapter Three

"Not Afraid of Any Two Men"

Jim Burrow in Montgomery, Ala., January 23, 1888.
Pinkerton Collection, Library of Congress.

Jim Burrow in Montgomery, Ala., January 23, 1888.
Pinkerton Collection, Library of Congress.

Toward the end of November, 1887, over a month after the second Benbrook robbery, William Brock received a letter in Erath County from Rube Burrow to meet him in Texarkana, Texas, on December 1. Burrow also asked him to write Henderson Brumley to join them, but Brumley turned out to be in Louisiana at the time and did not come.[146] Brock arrived in that town when scheduled, but the Burrow brothers did not show up for several more days. The men took rooms at the Cosmopolitan Hotel, near the St. Louis, Arkansas, and Texas Railroad depot, the railroad more familiarly known as the "Cotton Belt." Brock registered under his own name, but Jim signed in as "James Buchanan" and Rube as "Reuben Houston." Spending several days together, the three plotted their next train robbery. Both Brock and Jim were hesitant to pull a robbery because they were not familiar with the area and feared they might be caught. Rube took charge of the conversation, however, and convinced them it would be no more difficult than the earlier robberies. They assembled at the railroad roundhouse in Texarkana to finalize their plans.

The three men had only one pistol each, which they felt was not enough. On December 6 they took a train to the East Texas town of Tyler, in Smith County, but couldn't find the type of arms and cartridges they were after. Traveling on to Corsicana, in Navarro County, they purchased from merchant G.P. Keener two Winchester rifles and forty pounds of cartridges.[147] They returned to Texarkana on December 7. Brock bought through tickets for the three to go to Garland City, on the Miller County, Arkansas, line east of Texarkana where they planned to rob the train. Once there, however, they had to change that plan when they discovered a boarding train and a work force of men repairing the tracks at the spot where they wanted to stop the train. Walking to and spending the night a few miles further east at the Lewisville Station, they determined that the extent of water and mud from recent rains there made it unsuitable for a robbery. The three then trudged back and camped on December 8 near the Genoa Station, in Miller County about eight miles southeast of Texarkana. They intended to hold up the Cotton Belt train there that night, but the train went through without stopping, leaving the bandits without a chance to board it.

The three returned to their camp to figure out their next move. It was decided to follow the same procedure as in Texas: Rube would wait at the cut where the train was to be stopped, while Jim and Brock would go to Genoa and board the engine there just as the bell sounded signaling the departure of the train.[148] Because the weather was rainy, the three bandits wore dark rubber-cloth slicker coats. At about 6 p.m. on December 9, 1887, as the eastbound passenger train left the Genoa depot, Bill Brock and Jim Burrow, both masked, clambered aboard the engine, leveling their pistols at the engineer and fireman. The engineer declared that if they went ahead, they would collide with a southbound train expected momentarily. For some reason, Brock told him that the train was "side-tracked" and that there was no danger. The engineer cautiously moved the train eastward and stopped it where Rube was waiting at a cut. Jim called out to his brother, asking if the train was far enough, and Rube replied that it was.

Brock and Jim had the engineer and fireman leave the cab and they walked to the express car while Rube came toward them. Rube, whom the other robbers were calling "Cap," loudly demanded that the Southern Express Company messenger open the door. Upon the messenger's refusal, the outlaws fired some fifteen or twenty shots with Winchester rifles into the express car, at which time the express messenger doused the lights. Frustrated, the outlaws escorted the fireman back to the engine where a coal pick was procured. On return to the express car, Jim had the fireman attack the locked car door.[149]

The train's conductor, going with his lamp toward the engine to investigate why the train was stopped, had a bullet zip past his head, followed by another volley of rounds. He jumped back into a coach car, finding one bullet had gone through his coat under his arm. As in the other robberies, panic ensued among the passengers. The train's porter, realizing that a train robbery was in progress, leaped from the train and began running the several miles back to Genoa to report the robbery.

As the fireman battered the express car door, the express messenger, Thomas Cavin, realized that several lives were at stake and reluctantly opened it. Two robbers clambered aboard, lit a light, and searched the car. After finishing with the express car, they moved on to the mail car with their loot, including several sacks of silver. R.P. Johnson, the postal clerk, admitted them, noting that one of the intruders, identified as the leader of the band, was "much agitated," leading Johnson, without thinking, to tell the robber that he seemed more scared than he, Johnson, was. Johnson tried to impress on them that it was a federal offense to disturb the mails, and one robber responded, "That is so; we won't touch the mails." The three robbers then left on foot, hurrying off into the darkness.[150]

Carrying off their loot, about $2,800 in currency and $300 in silver, the bandits retreated about a mile into the nearby woods as the train departed, and built a fire in which to burn the express envelopes. The three then set out on foot for Texarkana to buy some whiskey and celebrate another successful job, Jim Burrow carrying the loot.

One account stated that a westbound freight train brought in news of the robbery about eight or nine o'clock that evening. Once notified, the Miller County sheriff immediately pulled together a posse in Texarkana and started for the scene in a special car provided by the railroad. Several other parties mounted and rode down the tracks, hoping to perhaps intercept the robbers.[151]

Following the railroad tracks, sometime after midnight, on a dirt road running parallel to the railroad tracks, the three robbers walked to within three or four miles of Texarkana when they ran into two men from the posse coming from Texarkana. The two lawmen spotted the three and ordered them to halt. The outlaws immediately opened fire. Uninjured, the lawmen emptied their pistols at the three, then hastily retreated to go back to Texarkana for more ammunition and help.[152] The bandits, likewise untouched by the lawmen's bullets, fled in the darkness, Jim and Brock shedding their cumbersome slickers, while Rube lost his light brown slouch hat and a cartridge box, all of which were later recovered by the posse.[153] The three men skirted Texarkana then split up at Sulphur Creek, Brock to return to Erath County and the Burrow brothers to go back to Alabama.[154]

In the early hours of December 10, the general superintendent of the St. Louis, Arkansas, and Texas Railway, W.P. Homan, wired Arkansas Governor Simon Hughes about the robbery, advising him that the railroad had initiated several posses in the area.[155] Governor Hughes promptly wired the Miller County Sheriff in Texarkana declaring a $200 reward for the arrest and conviction of each of the three robbers, and the railroad also offered a large reward.[156] As with the aftermath of the Texas robberies, suspects throughout the area were stopped and investigated, and sometimes arrested, by lawmen.[157]

The Southern Express Company, the victim of the robbery, was not of a mind to leave the matter to the local authorities. Formed at the outset of the Civil War, the company initially existed to provide express services for southern states.[158] In 1875, when train robbery had become more the vogue among outlaws, the company had urged its agents and messengers to arm themselves, offering to "suitably reward" any employee who killed a robber.[159] In 1879, when several train robbers victimized the Southern Express Company in a train holdup at Union City, Tennessee, the express company turned to the Pinkerton Detective Agency, which promptly caught all the participants. After the Genoa robbery, the express company telegraphed the Pinkertons in Chicago, once again seeking their expertise. J.C. McGinn, the agent assigned by William Pinkerton, was on the ground at Genoa on December 12.[160]

The primary clues for the detective were the two slickers and hat abandoned by the train robbers after their encounter with the possemen. The hat had a label from a merchant in Dublin, Texas, Utterbach and Davis, located in Erath County. Both slickers, which were new, had the cost mark "K.W.P." imprinted. The Pinkerton detectives and federal lawmen hastened to Dublin, but the purchaser of the hat could not be recalled by the store, it having sold hundreds of that type. No one could be located at Dublin familiar with the slickers, and the detectives fanned out to see if they could locate who sold them. Merchants were checked as far away as Corsicana and Waco, as well as at Stephenville and other neighboring communities. In Stephenville, a clerk at Fry & Jordan's store recalled selling such a coat to a man named Granger, who lived in Dublin and had a bad reputation.[161] However, finally, south of Stephenville and due east of Dublin, in the tiny Erath County town of Alexander, a clerk at the firm of Sherman & Talwell identified the cost mark on the coats as one that he himself had affixed. Reflecting for a few seconds, he recalled selling a coat like that to Bill Brock, whose father-in-law lived only about five miles from there on the road to Dublin. He also recalled that when Brock bought the coat, the clerk sold another to a man accompanying Brock, a man who afterwards went to Alabama. He also thought that Brock had been away to Texarkana.

The detective had previously made a list of names found on Texarkana hotel registers and noted that Bill Brock had signed in under his own name. Another detective, on his way to Dublin with the Genoa engineer, spotted a man on the train leaving Waco who the engineer said fit the description of one of the train robbers. He followed the man to Dublin, in Erath County, and, after comparing notes, it was determined that the man was Bill Brock and that there was sufficient evidence upon which to base his arrest. The investigation also established that Brock had two friends, Rube and Jim Burrow, whose description fit those of the other robbers at Genoa.[162] More incriminating, Brock had met his wife at Waco and the two went on a shopping spree with his share of the loot. They packed two new trunks with their purchases and returned to Erath County.[163]

While Brock and his wife were returning, the Burrow brothers decided to briefly go back home to Lamar County, Alabama. They arrived there on December 20, and on the 29th Rube sent a letter to Brock stating that all was well and offering to sell him the Burrow farm in Erath County for $700.[164] But lawmen were already on the move in Texas. At about three o'clock on the morning of Saturday, December 31, 1887, and with arrest warrants in hand, Detective McGinn, Deputy U.S. Marshal J.M. Waller, and local lawmen surrounded Brock's log cabin five miles from Dublin. The lawmen slid quietly through the front door and confronted Ben Acker, Brock's father-in-law, who told them that Brock and a man named Singleton were in the next room asleep. The heavily-armed detectives awakened Brock and took him into custody without any resistance, although he had a loaded 45-caliber revolver beneath his pillow. He was promptly taken by train to Waco, where he was held in a room in the Pacific Hotel, then taken the next day to Texarkana. While waiting for the train at Waco, a man named Pittman told Detective McGinn that he had heard from a Dublin physician that the doctor had seen Rube Burrow's children playing with twenty-dollar gold coins right after the Gordon robbery.[165] This would have been difficult, of course, because the children were almost certainly in Alabama. Brock was confronted by the Cotton Belt engineer and others who identified him, and he promptly confessed his part in the Genoa robbery and identified the Burrow brothers as his cohorts, as well as Brumley and Thornton also being involved in the Texas robberies. With all of the information that had been gathered, Rube and Jim Burrow were now fugitives for the first time, although it is likely they believed that the lawmen had no idea who they were.

On January 5, 1888, Detective McGinn and two of his Pinkerton operatives, with requisition papers in hand from the Arkansas governor, left Texarkana for Fayette, Alabama, the county seat of the county immediately east of Lamar County, and some twenty miles from Vernon. They first stopped at Montgomery to obtain state arrest warrants for the Burrow brothers. At Fayette, the detective sent a message to Fillmore Pennington, the sheriff of Lamar County, to meet with him at Fayette. The sheriff met with the party and told them that he knew the brothers and that the last time they returned to Vernon they spent money in purchasing property and horses. Satisfied the sheriff could be trusted, the party then left at about three in the afternoon of Sunday the 8th, riding to Vernon through continuous rains with a pine torch for light, and arriving about ten that evening. Staying at the local hotel and posing as "mineralists" looking for iron ore, they spent Monday entertaining eager queries from local citizens about specimens and mining opportunities available on their respective premises, the "mineralists" promising to personally inspect those properties. It had been surmised that the Burrow brothers might show themselves in Vernon, but the heavy rains all day long foreclosed that likelihood.

Pennington sent a deputy to scout out where the brothers might be located, and reported to the detectives that Rube was probably staying with his father and that Jim had recently purchased a place where he had set up housekeeping. It was decided that the detectives should make a raid on Jim Burrow's house with hopes of perhaps running across both fugitives.

Well before dawn on the morning of Tuesday, January 10, 1888, McGinn shared a wagon with Sheriff Pennington and Pinkerton detectives Williams and W.J. Wilbosky, while detectives Carney and Wing were on horseback. The party relied on one of Pennington's deputies, named Jerry, to guide them to Jim Burrow's place.[166] Arriving just before dawn at a point the guide said was about a half-mile from Burrow's farmhouse, the posse slowly surrounded the structure. As the party moved in and the sun was peeking over the horizon, the guide suddenly told them that he was mistaken and Burrow lived in another house about a half mile from there. At the second house, the deputy confessed that he was again mistaken. Now daylight, the detectives decided that the element of surprise was gone and considered returning to Vernon before they were discovered, but residents in the second house were up and could be seen looking at the party. The deputy claimed that Jim Burrow's house was another two miles further. The detectives decided that their cover was blown and to await another twenty-for hours to conduct its raid would be useless. So they committed to going ahead and trying the raid in daylight, hoping that the element of surprise was still with them.

Pressing on, stopping only briefly to interrogate a man named Thompson they encountered walking near them, the group finally came to the house indicated by Deputy Jerry, and the lawmen deployed and advanced. The house belonged to Martha Ann Hankins, Jim's mother-in-law, who he was visiting. When the lawmen were within about one hundred yards of the house, the detectives heard a tearing sound in the structure's rear. Jim Burrow had spotted them and, with a pistol in each hand, ran out the rear, pushing the rear door so violently that it came off its hinges. The detectives opened fire with their rifles at the fleeing fugitive, some of the bullets even perforating his clothing, but he reached the cover of the woods and escaped capture unharmed.[167] McGinn had drawn a steady bead on the fleeing fugitive with his Winchester, but was diverted from firing when one of the lawmen said they had nabbed Burrow, only to discover it was another man who was staying there. For the first time, Rube and Jim's family and neighbors were now aware that the two brothers were train robbers, wanted in two states.

While the detectives were trying to flush Jim, Rube was visiting at Kennedy, some eighteen miles southeast of Vernon. Family members, alerted to the presence of the detectives when the sleuths came to Allen Burrow's house to search it, dispatched Henry Cash, a soon-to-be in-law, who met Rube and told him what had happened. The detectives searched Allen Burrow's house, and were told truthfully that Rube had gone to Kennedy. Rube waited on the road outside Kennedy while Cash rode on in to town, where he was making arrangements for his marriage the next day to one of Rube's sisters. When Cash returned, the two rode back to Vernon, skirting the main road, where they covertly met Burrow's father and brother Jim near the house of Green Harris. At midnight, Rube and Jim quietly rode out of Lamar County, now aware that they were wanted men.[168]

Twelve days later, on the evening of Sunday, January 22, 1888, after hiding out in various remote places, the two brothers ventured out and boarded the southbound train at Brock's Gap, twelve miles south of Birmingham, headed for Montgomery. They were occupying a "double seat" when the conductor, J.S. Callahan, came by to collect their fare. One of the men pulled out a big roll of cash to pay for the tickets, and, afterwards, Callahan saw one of the men pull out a six-shooter, remove the cartridges, then reload the pistol, saying, "I guess we are fixed now." His suspicions about them increased when one of the men said, "Look out for the Junction," as the train rumbled to a brief stop at Calera. Callahan ordered the porter, Osborn Cleveland, to keep an eye on the two suspicious men, who were now lying down in the seats apparently trying to sleep, while he stepped off the train at Calera and wired Police Chief Adolphus Gerald in Montgomery to have a special officer meet the train.[169] As the train approached Montgomery, Callahan told the engineer not to stop until he got to the depot in order to prevent the two men from getting off in the railyard before reaching the station.

When the train pulled into the Montgomery depot about eight p.m., Police Captain John W. Martin was on hand to greet it. Callahan met the officer and said that he thought the two men on his train were suspicious and ought to be checked out. Martin called to an officer on duty at the depot, McGee, to assist him. Both officers had their uniforms obscured by raincoats and slouch hats to protect against the rain. Rube and Jim alit from the train and started walking back down the track. Martin, assuming the demeanor of a railroad man, hailed them, "You can't go through that railroad cut at night." Rube responded that they intended to go into the country to buy timber, but were looking for a second-class hotel for the night. Thinking quickly, the captain responded that he and his companion were going into town and would take him to the "Gerald House." The four men, followed by another officer, Carrigan, walked about half a mile and, on reaching the police station, Martin inserted a key to unlock the door. Rube asked, "What place is this?" Shoving the door half open and grabbing Rube by the arm, Martin replied, "This is the office of the chief of police, and you boys may consider yourselves under arrest."[170]

Rube yanked his arm away, responding, "Well, I guess you won't!" Carrigan and McGee grabbed Jim, who was wearing a large slouch cowboy hat, trying to subdue him. Martin wrestled with Rube, scuffling at the entrance, when the door to the station, which was on a spring, closed on Martin's raincoat. Before Martin could open the door to get loose, Rube had managed to tear loose and run across the street. Martin got out of his coat and started after Rube. Jim managed to get loose from the two officers scuffling with him, but as he ran he tripped over a hydrant and fell into the street. The officers were quickly on him and he was taken securely into custody.

After briefly watching his brother struggling with the officers, Rube raced to get away, Officer McGee and a Sergeant Murphy in pursuit. McGee got off one shot at him, missing, and Rube began increasing the distance between them. As he ran, a compositor for the *Montgomery Advertiser*, Cornelius Hartford "Neil" Bray, 29, was walking on the other side of the street. Murphy called out, "Catch him," and Bray started to head the fugitive off. Seeing that he could not outrun his new pursuer, Rube changed course and ran at Bray. He pulled his pistol and shot at the young man twice, the first round missing and the second shot entering his left lung. Bray sank to the street crying out, "He has got me." Rube continued to run, finally losing the pursuing officers in the town's labyrinth of streets. The officers quickly got a hack to carry Bray to the station and sought medical help, certain that his wounds were mortal, although he eventually recovered.[171]

Taken upstairs in the police station, Jim gave his name as "Hankins," but a search of his person turned up an envelope addressed to "R.H. Burrow," postmarked from Jacksonville, Texas, as well as $175 in gold coins, $173 in paper currency, and a number of .45-caliber cartridges, although he had no weapon. The pants that he wore were new, the tag from the Birmingham store where they were purchased still affixed. The authorities assumed that he was Rube and the escaping fugitive was Jim. At first claiming that "I ain't Rube Burrow," Jim said, "I could tell a heap if I wanted, but accordin' to the old saying I guess I had better keep my mouth shut."[172]

Into the morning hours of the next day, police combed the countryside looking for the fugitive. Both the Pinkertons and the Southern Express Company wired the Montgomery Police asking that their prisoner be held at all cost, recommending that he be securely ironed. On Monday afternoon, Jim was escorted to a photograph gallery where his picture was taken, both with and without his large hat. Continuing to be reticent, he promised to behave if the officers removed his irons once he was in his cell, which they did. He then claimed to be Reuben Burrow and that it was Jim that shot Bray and escaped.

At about nine p.m., Monday, January 23, three Montgomery police officers out searching the countryside were informed that the man they were seeking was staying at the cabin of a black man named Brady, near the Tippecanoe Station on the Western Railway, about seven miles from Montgomery. Calling on a citizen, Tom Judkins, to help them, the officers surrounded the cabin as best they could and sent an elderly black woman in to try and decoy him outside. She quickly returned to the officers, reporting that he had a pistol "most as long as a gun," and refused to go back. Inside, Rube gathered his effects, except for an overcoat left behind, and with his boots held in his left hand and his pistol in the other, he jumped through a window and ran toward a marsh thirty yards off. He ran near Officer Luke Hill who got off five shots at him without effect. Officer Bolling Young, who had a shotgun, discharged a load of buckshot at the running man. Rube put his arm up to cover his head, although the shot may have hit his side as he was seen to flinch. He dropped his boots as he ran. Young reloaded his shotgun, although with smaller gauge shot, and mounted his horse to pursue the fleeing fugitive. Crossing the marsh, Rube made it to the railroad track, turned, and fired four shots at Young, who threw himself down on one side of the horse Indian style. The officer cut loose with another charge, which was believed to have peppered Rube's face. Rube then disappeared into the nearby swamp and the officers gave up the chase because of darkness. Additional officers, as well as a pack of dogs, were rushed to the scene to expand the search.[173] The abandoned boots were taken back to Montgomery and shown to Jim, but he refused to identify them.[174]

On Tuesday morning, January 24, the officers found that an old blind horse had been stolen from Brady, and assumed it was taken by Rube. Riding bare backed, bare footed, and without a coat in the wet January cold, it was thought that he would not be hard to track down. However, in spite of efforts throughout the area to find him, he once more disappeared. In Montgomery, Jim remained quiet, still insisting that he was Rube. At one point he coyly said, "Well, to tell the truth, I hardly know what my real name is. I have been called both Reub and Jim Burrows, John Hankins, Bill Jones and several other names and I have become so muddled I don't know what my name is." The Southern Express Company commenced garnishment proceedings to gain possession of the money found on Jim.

Agee melodramatically painted a harrowing ordeal faced by Rube Burrow in the freezing swamps, which probably was close to the truth:

> Hatless and bare-footed, the friendless felon now found himself, at dark of night, in a wilderness of swamp, whose treacherous waters were covered with a tangled growth of brush and vines, and chilled with the winter's cold. Exhausted with the toils of the day's flight, his face and neck smarting with the keen pain of the wounds he had just received, hungry and foot-sore, his body quivering with the biting cold—could human flesh and blood be subjected to the frenzy of sharper distress than that which faced Rube as he blindly picked his footing through this *terra incognita*?[175]

At some point in his flight, according to Agee, Rube came upon a warm cabin in which slept an African-American family. Sneaking in, he quietly warmed himself in front of a fire without waking the family. When he had rested, he stole some shoes and a blanket and resumed his journey, stopping at a nearby stable only long enough to steal another horse. He had again successfully eluded his pursuers.[176]

In Dallas, Jim and Ben Hughes, who had been previously convicted and given life sentences for complicity in the Gordon robbery, were tried on January 25, along with Harvey Carter, in the federal court for willfully obstructing the passage of the mail during the Bellevue robbery in December 1886. Only three witnesses were called by the United States Attorney, all of whom testified that these were not the men who held up the Bellevue train in December 1886. The engineer who testified, when asked what he was doing while the robbery was going on, responded, "I was standing up, being robbed like the rest of the damned fools." The judge instructed the jury to return a verdict of not guilty, and fifteen minutes after the trial began, it was over. The Hughes brother were still held pending the appeal of their prior conviction, and Carter was held to face a murder charge in Palo Pinto County.[177]

Rube slowly made his way through the woods, swamps, and backroads of Alabama. On Tuesday, January 24, about eleven miles from Montgomery, he spent the night in a "small outhouse," requesting food and fire from the black occupants who were too terrified to help him. When he left about nine the next morning, he ate with great relish some bread he had begged from two children on the place. For about an hour, he paced the Western Railroad track as if he did not know where he was going, then he disappeared again into the swamp. Alerted, a search party of policemen looked over the area, finding the fugitive's footprints leading into the swamp, but heavy rains had made roads impassable and they returned to Montgomery Wednesday evening. Telegrams continued to come in reporting sightings of men resembling the wanted fugitive,[178] but the general conclusion was that he had been successful in eluding the authorities and was gone.

By now, after matching known descriptions, the Montgomery authorities were pretty sure that their prisoner was Jim, not Rube Burrow. He continued to try to confound his captors, telling them that he was raised in Perry County, that he thought his father was dead, and that he knew nothing of the Texas robberies or anything else that might incriminate him. "I am a great coward," he continued in his sarcasm, "and that other man that the officers are trying to capture— he is a coward, too. We are both big cowards. There are two things in this world that I am very much afraid of; that's a rattlesnake and a mad dog."

When asked where he got his big hat, Jim responded, "I beat another man guessing for that hat." When the comment was not understood, he explained, "Well, it was this way. The other man guessed that I would pay for it, and I guessed I wouldn't. That is the way I got it." He claimed to know Alabama Governor Thomas Seay personally, proclaiming him one of the best men in that section of the country. Captain Martin observed that, while uneducated, Jim was very far from being a fool, possessing "lots of horse sense and backwoods shrewdness." His photographs were posted outside the police station so people could see this recent sensation in the city.[179] On Thursday morning, in the custody of Pinkerton detective W.J. Wilbosky and Captain Martin, Jim was hustled aboard a train, arriving Friday evening at Texarkana, Arkansas, where he joined Brock, then suffering from pneumonia, both of them to face charges for the Genoa robbery.[180] While aboard the train, Jim finally admitted his true identity. "I am Jim Burrow, and the other man is my brother Rube, and if you give us two pistols apiece we are not afraid of any two men living."[181]

In the meantime, the authorities were moving quickly in Texas. Bill Brock had revealed everything he knew about the Burrow brothers, the train robberies, and the rest of the gang. Detectives and lawmen began to round them up. Pinkerton detectives, accompanied by Fort Worth City Marshal Sam Farmer, made their way on Tuesday, January 24, to Erath County and the home in Alexander of Henderson Brumley. In the early hours of Wednesday morning, he was taken into custody without resistance and hurriedly taken to Fort Worth. The officers recovered $1,200 in cash from him. Marshal Farmer requested of the local press that nothing be published about the arrest until Nep Thornton and Harrison Askey had also been apprehended, and Brumley was secreted at the Mansion Hotel rather than placed in jail. On Friday afternoon, however, Fort Worth attorney John Templeton applied for a writ of habeas corpus on Brumley's behalf, and a temporary bond was set at $3,000, which Brumley's sureties were able to post.[182] He was then registered at the Pickwick Hotel in Fort Worth, as was U.S. Marshal Cabell and several Pinkerton detectives.[183] At a hearing on the writ Saturday morning, January 28, before state District Judge Robert E. Beckham,[184] the state did not introduce any evidence and Brumley was discharged. However, before he could leave the courthouse, he was greatly surprised when he was immediately rearrested on three federal warrants charging him with complicity in the Gordon and two Benbrook robberies. Once more in irons, he was quickly transported by Marshal Cabell to Dallas.[185]

Then a bizarre episode occurred. On Saturday, while Brumley was being hustled off to Dallas, his attorney, Templeton, filed a civil lawsuit in Tarrant County against the Pacific Express Company, the company's agent T.N. Edgell, Pinkerton detectives John McGinn, E.H. Wing, and E.F. Carney, Marshal Sam Farmer, and J.N. Williams of Bowie County. Asking over $50,000 in damages, Brumley asserted that when the lawmen came to his home in Erath County, where his wife had "been recently confined in childbirth, and was then in a dangerous condition," they shot into the house, as well as shot at Brumley's brother who was a guest there. He further alleged that when he was taken into custody and held at the Mansion Hotel, the detectives assaulted and beat him.[186] Farmer responded to the press that "hardly any of the allegations" were true, and the defendants' formal response to the lawsuit primarily complained about the money damages being sought.[187] The case lingered without action until November 7, 1889, when it was dismissed because Brumley failed to give a bond to cover court costs, as ordered by the court.[188]

In Dallas on Monday morning, January 30, 1888, the United States Commissioner set an $11,000 bond for Brumley's appearance at an examining trial approximately two weeks later. Posting the bond, he returned home to his family in Erath County the next day.[189] At the same time, the law enforcement authorities were still at work. On the evening of the 29th, Marshal Cabell and Stephens County Sheriff John J. Douglass arrested Harrison Askey at his home seven miles west of Breckinridge and took him to Dallas, where he was bound over for the action of the grand jury with bail set at $2,500, an amount his bondmen were finally able to raise on February 6.[190]

On Wednesday, February 1, 1888, in the Texarkana, Arkansas, court of Miller County Justice of the Peace McFlinn, the examining trial of Bill Brock and Jim Burrow began behind closed doors, lasting two days. Jim was described as having a "careless air" and a smile, which changed to nervous twitching as the examination of witnesses progressed. The express agent on the Genoa train positively identified the two defendants, recalling that it was Jim who ordered a can of oil to be brought in order to burn the express car. Brock testified, giving a full account of what happened. At the conclusion of the hearing, Judge McFlinn set a surprisingly low bond of $750 for Brock, and a steep $7,500 bond for Jim Burrow. Jim couldn't come up with any cash and was ordered to the prison at Little Rock to be held for safekeeping until his trial was scheduled, the Miller County Jail being deemed too insecure. The low bond for Brock led to speculation that he was secretly a Pinkerton agent who had been assigned to infiltrate the Burrow gang, a claim that was promptly denied by the detective agency. While Jim was being escorted to Little Rock, two merchants stepped forward to provide Brock's bond, and detectives promptly whisked him off to Dallas.[191]

Arriving at Little Rock, Jim finally made a full admission of his guilt in the Genoa robbery except as to the amount of money taken, and he would not implicate anyone else other than Brock. He told the detectives he regretted not killing Brock when, some three days after the Genoa robbery, he claimed he found a letter in Brock's pocket outlining the robbery and naming all concerned.[192] Jim's brother-in-law, James Cash, left Vernon, Alabama, on Tuesday, February 14, to visit him in jail at Little Rock.[193]

In Washington D.C., the spate of train robberies in the western states had given rise to concern over the safety of postal employees. On February 4, at the behest of the Railway Mail Service, the Post Office Department announced that postal employees on railroad routes thought most susceptible to robbery would be armed at government expense. Thus they would be "prepared to successfully defend themselves and mails from attacks of these 'road agents' however skillfully planned or unexpectedly made."[194]

Brumley's examining trial commenced in the United States Commissioner's court in Dallas on Tuesday, February 14, 1888, with twenty-nine witnesses lined up by United States Attorney Charles B. Pearre. The defense, on the other hand, presented witnesses to establish an alibi for the defendant. At the conclusion of the hearing on Friday, the 17th, Brumley's bond was set at $15,000 and he was placed in jail to await the action of the grand jury.[195]

Pinkerton detectives returned to Texarkana on February 22 with Brock in tow, spiriting him into a hotel under the name of Lawrence, although he was recognized by a newsman. It was discovered that the group had booked train passage to St. Louis, kicking off renewed speculation that Brock was really a Pinkerton operative.[196] On the 25th, the Pinkertons broadcast a reward circular offering $700 for the arrest and conviction of Rube Burrow for the Genoa robbery.[197] This reward was in addition to those already offered by the states of Texas and Arkansas, as well as the various railroads and express companies involved. Coincidentally, the Cotton Belt was again held up on the 29th, twenty miles south of Pine Bluff by three men, but not the Burrow gang, and who, after setting the express car afire to force admittance, got away with about $13,000.[198]

The federal grand jury for the Northern District of Texas, convening at Graham in Young County on March 15, heard the prosecution's evidence, including the testimony of Harrison Askey, and returned an indictment against Askey, Henderson Brumley, Nep

Thornton, and Rube and Jim Burrow for conspiring to rob the mails at Gordon.[199] Further, Brumley was indicted by himself for assaulting postal agent Richard Griffim in the June 1887 Benbrook robbery.[200] The grand jury also returned an indictment against Brock and the two Burrow brothers for making an assault on Griffin at Benbrook.[201] At the same time, on March 28, the Hughes brothers, Ben and Jim, who had won a new trial in an appeal from the life sentence imposed for the Gordon robbery, were acquitted based on their alibi evidence and probably the statements of Brock and Askey.[202] A total of $37,500 in bonds was imposed against Brumley, which his bondmen were able to post.[203]

Rube Burrow not having surfaced since his escape at Montgomery, his father, Allen, decided to come to Montgomery to search for his son's body, assuming he had perished in the swamps. He freely spoke to the press about both of his boys, recalling that they had always behaved and never showed any bad character traits. "My boys never told me the history of their lives in Texas and I have learned more since I have been here in Montgomery than I ever knew before. I can hardly believe my senses."[204] Although he asked the authorities for the money taken from Jim when he was arrested for the support of his grandchildren, the Southern Express Company had already filed a garnishment action to seize it as loot from the Genoa robbery.[205] When he returned to Lamar County, Allen Burrow praised the Montgomery police for their courtesies.[206] Any search for Rube Burrow was fruitless, because he was already a long way from there.

Chapter Four

"Butch, I Am Done For"

John Thomas Burrow and family. Courtesy Floyd
Mack Morris, Jr., Sulligent, Alabama.

Train robber Eugene Franklin Bunch. Texas Collection, Baylor University.

Reuben Smith. Post Office Department Records, National Archives.

Leonard C. Brock alias "Joe Jackson." George Agee, Rube Burrow:
King of Outlaws. Chicago: The Henneberry CO., 1890.

Moses J. and Mary Jane Graves. Courtesy Clanton Dubose, Vernon, Alabama.

Despite the bad weather and formidable swamps and countryside, Rube Burrow finally made it back to Lamar County and the protection of his family. For the first time he learned what had happened to his brother and the perfidy of Bill Brock, likely talking to brother-in-law James Cash who had gone to Little Rock to visit Jim. A plan to rescue Jim began to form in Rube's mind, one which he could not carry out alone; he needed help.

In the spring of 1886, when Rube and Bill Brock were in Cooke County, in North Texas, they had hired a 26-year-old man who called himself Lewis Waldrip to help round up livestock. The party traveled through Young and Wise Counties, finally selling cattle at Fort Worth, at which time Rube quit the cattle business and discharged Waldrip. While in Fort Worth, Waldrip was accosted by a bully who kept bothering him. When Waldrip told the man he wanted no more of his talk, the two cursed each other and the bully pulled a knife. Waldrip struck the man on the arm with his pistol, knocking the knife out of the man's hand. Rube Burrow watched as Waldrip then knocked the bully to the ground, the encounter leaving a favorable impression in Burrow's mind.[207]

In actuality, Waldrip was Leonard Calvert Brock, who was no relation to Bill Brock. The 28-year-old Brock stood about five feet eight inches and weighed a slender 105 pounds. Prominent scars were noticeable on his forehead and left cheek, and he was reticent to look someone in the eyes when talking.[208] After leaving Burrow, "Waldrip" roamed across the state, and on into Louisiana, Alabama, and Florida doing odd jobs. In the latter part of 1887 he went to Sherman in North Texas. It was here, in February of 1888, that he said he received a letter from Rube at Vernon stating that Rube was in some sort of trouble and asking "Waldrip" to come meet with him. "Waldrip" replied in a letter to James Cash in Vernon that he was undecided, but received another letter urging him to come.[209] Finally, around the first of March 1888, he went to Sulligent, Alabama, then made his way south twelve miles to Allen Burrow's home near Vernon. Rube was at James Cash's place, and there he told Leonard Brock what had happened at Montgomery and the two agreed to work together while Rube sought to evade the detectives looking for him.

According to Leonard Brock, the two stayed in Lamar County about a week, then made their way cross country, detouring through

Mississippi, to Baldwin County in the southern tip of Alabama on its border with the Florida Panhandle where they were well secluded from any snooping detectives. Here they went to work at Dunnaway's log camp, Brock driving a log team, and Rube, under the alias of Ward, working for a man named John Barnes sawing logs. After about a month they were discharged and worked for a few days at another logging camp. The two traveled back to Mississippi on foot, finally pulling together enough money to purchase horses. By May of 1888 they had returned to Lamar County, staying hidden near Jim Cash's farm until early August.[210]

In some manner, Rube received information that his brother would be taken from the Little Rock prison and returned to Texarkana for trial around September 5. Rube was hellbent on rescuing his brother, and Brock agreed to assist him, "even if we had to kill them to do so." Saddling up, they set out for Arkansas. They made their way, arriving at Donaldson, fifteen miles south of Malvern, which was about half way between Little Rock and Texarkana, where they planned to take Jim from the train. On the off chance that Jim might be found on other trains, they rode to Curtis, south of Arkadelphia, where they looked through several trains. They learned that a train due through there would not stop, but would go on to Arkadelphia, so they raced back to Arkadelphia, Rube vowing to kill his horse from the endeavor if necessary. However, they just missed the train as they rode into town. Finally coming to the conclusion that theirs was an impossible mission, Rube and Brock gave up the rescue scheme and headed east.

About the first of October, they crossed the Mississippi River at Helena, Arkansas, and went to work picking cotton for farmer Fletcher Stephens in Tate County, about eighteen miles from the county seat of Senatobia on the Illinois Central line, for board and fifty cents per hundred pounds. Rube adopted the name of Charlie, and Brock went as "Henry Davis."[211] Occasionally they went off into nearby swamps to practice shooting. Quitting around the first of December, the two now determined to rob a train, apparently tired of the roaming life.[212] Perhaps thinking of Texas train robber Sam Bass and his trusty lieutenant, Frank Jackson, who disappeared after the gang was shot up by Texas Rangers in Round Rock in July of 1878, Rube dubbed his new partner "Joe Jackson."[213]

While Rube and "Joe Jackson" were traveling across the southeast, the turmoil in Texas had yet to be played out. On the evening of Thursday, May 3, 1888, in Stephens County, about twenty miles north of Cisco, Harrison Askey, while out on bond, was near his home rounding up some stray cows when two masked men on horseback raced up to him and took him away at gunpoint in a southeasterly direction. His wife saw what happened and caused an alarm to be raised in the community. A posse with bloodhounds was formed and pursuit continued until darkness fell. The hunt resumed on Friday morning and a trail was followed several miles south toward Merriman, in Eastland County, when the posse encountered O.P. Watson of Ranger. He told the pursuers that Askey had been at his house earlier that morning and that Watson had loaned him a horse on which to go home, after exacting assurance that Askey was telling the truth.

Askey was finally located and stated that he could not recognize the men, and that they had told him that they were taking him to a "crowd of men" not far off who wanted him. The two men rode on either side of him for about twenty miles in the direction of Palo Pinto County, guarding him closely, Askey said. At one point in the southeast part of Eastland County, he said that they had to ride through a narrow gap in a mountainous area single file and the two men rode in front of him. He quietly slipped off his horse and hid in some nearby woods until they were out of sight, the riderless horse continuing behind the men. Discovering that Askey was missing, the two men returned but could not find their escaped prisoner, finally giving up the search and leaving. Staying hidden until Saturday morning, Askey said he made his way to Ranger where he reported what happened. He later claimed that upon returning home on Watson's horse, the same two men reappeared, but he outrode them and escaped again.

Askey later stated that he had a suspicion that one of them was a man named Miller. The immediate speculation, however, was that Askey was to be murdered to prevent his testimony against Brumley, Thornton, and the Burrow brothers, but Askey, probably out of fear, declined to cooperate.[214]

An examining trial was held for Nep Thornton, who had finally been arrested at Alexander and brought to Dallas on May 28, before the United States Commissioner in Dallas from May 30 through Friday, June 1. He was bound over for grand jury consideration, and a $6,000 bond was set, which he apparently made.[215] But then both Brumley and Thornton suddenly jumped bond, Brumley failing to appear for a hearing on the 4th. The next day the court issued a capias warrant for his arrest.[216] On Wednesday, June 6, Brumley's bonds, totaling an aggregate of $26,500, were declared forfeited, much to the consternation of his bondsmen.[217] Officers, as well as some of the fugitives' bondsmen, congregated at Cisco in Eastland County to commence the search for Brumley and Thornton.[218] A deputy sheriff and posse from Stephens County encountered the two on Sunday, June 10, near Thornton's home eight miles from Breckinridge and they exchanged shots. Blood was found on the trail of the escaping outlaws, indicating that one of the men or their horses had been hit.[219] Finally on July 19, aware that he was wanted dead or alive, Brumley surrendered to his bondsmen without explaining why he fled. He claimed to know nothing of the whereabouts of Thornton, who continued to be at large.[220]

Both Brumley and Thornton were again indicted in federal court on October 19, 1888, this time for kidnapping Askey, alleging they conspired to "deter by force and intimidation" any testimony against them. It was claimed that the two had threatened to kill Askey, extorting a promise that he would leave the country in three days and hide from the officers sent after him.[221] Brumley immediately responded with alibi evidence, reasserting in defense that Askey had told others he did not know who kidnapped him.

On August 2, Bill Brock was returned to Texarkana, having been with the Pinkertons in Chicago. Assuming they would be indicted by Miller County, his trial and that of Jim Burrow was scheduled to commence in September. Jim was brought from the prison in Little Rock. It was already speculated that, upon conviction, Jim would receive a severe sentence and Brock would be convicted then pardoned by the Arkansas governor. Brock was jailed rather than allowed to roam the city out of fear of an assassination attempt by friends of the Burrows.[222] On September 4, the grand jury for Miller County, Arkansas, returned three state indictments each against Bill Brock and the Burrow brothers, one for the Genoa robbery and two for attempted murder during the robbery. Although trial was scheduled for the 11th, a continuance until March was granted at the request of Jim's lawyer so he could summon witnesses from Alabama in his client's behalf in order to prove an alibi.[223]

Returned to the prison at Little Rock, and in spite of having confessed his own part in the robbery, Jim decided to undergo a jury trial anyway and plead not guilty. Physically ailing from a malarial fever, on September 4 he wrote James Cash and his wife in Alabama, asking them to send money to his lawyers to pay for his defense.[224]

Jim was sicker than he thought and was admitted to the prison hospital on September 20. Soon his malarial condition, diagnosed as typhoid, degenerated into delirium, and for close to a week he raved incoherently. He died in the Little Rock prison on October 5, 1888, and was buried on prison grounds.[225] Jim Burrow having died, Bill Brock went on trial in Texarkana on December 12, pleading guilty to the state charge of grand larceny of the express company, but not guilty to the two attempted murder charges. His wife, Elizabeth, attended the trial and seemed "deeply distressed." On the 13th, the jury found him guilty of the theft charge and assessed a prison term of three years. He was found not guilty on one of the assault charges, and the other was quashed by the court.[226] Brock was immediately taken to the prison at Little Rock, confident that he would be pardoned and that Marshal W.L. Cabell could use his services in tracking down Nep Thornton and other train robbers.[227] A request was promptly made by federal prosecutor Pearre in Texas to Arkansas Governor Hughes to pardon Bill Brock because of his value as a material witness in the Benbrook and Gordon robberies. Pearre also wrote U.S. Attorney General W.H.H. Miller that Brock was willing to plead guilty to one of the Benbrook robberies in return for a five-year sentence, and urged the Attorney General to exert what influence he could to gain the pardon.[228]

Rube Burrow and "Joe Jackson" had selected their target: the Illinois Central at the small Mississippi village of Duck Hill, located in Montgomery County in the middle of the state, twelve miles south of Grenada. First settled about 1834, tradition holds that the hill for which the small town was named stemmed from a Choctaw Indian who lived on the hill and called himself Chief Duck.[229] The two men arrived shortly after dark on December 15, 1888. "Jackson" bought some sardines at a store then walked back to where their horses were hitched about half a mile north of town, east of the track, and the two waited for the train as the cold and rain enveloped them

Just before ten p.m., with rain falling, the northbound Illinois Central passenger train pulled into Duck Hill for its customary two-minute stop. As the engine left, beginning to pick up steam, the two men, masked, leaped aboard the engine cab. The engineer, Albert J. Law, began to stop the train to put off what he thought were tramps, but the two men, revolvers in hand, ordered him to "run her like hell" until told to stop. About eight hundred yards north of the station, amidst marshy swamps, the train was halted. "Jackson" stepped off the train and fired a shot in the air to intimidate any passengers who might get brave. Inside the train, the conductor, P.B. Wilkerson, rushed through the ladies coach and smoking car to find out why the train stopped. As the conductor stepped to the ground, Engineer Law hollered at him to go back or he would be killed. Wilkerson reentered the cars and called on any of the passengers to help him stop the robbery. About half a dozen men agreed to help him, but one man gruffly said, "Sit down, you fools; if you go out there you'll get killed!"

One man stepped forward anyway, 32-year-old Robert Chester Hughes from Jackson, Tennessee, who went by Chester. Aboard with him were his sister and her two children, accompanying him back to Jackson.[230] Hughes borrowed a Winchester from another passenger and went through the smoking car with Wilkerson, who had a pistol. Outside, with the help of the express messenger, W.H. Harris, Rube climbed into the express car, which the messenger had opened to see why the train stopped. "Jackson" remained on the ground guarding the engineer and the fireman. Wilkerson called out through the darkness to the engineer, "Law, where are you?" When Law responded, the conductor warned him that he was about to shoot. All of a sudden, the engineer took off running as Wilkerson and Hughes opened fire. A Traveling Passenger Agent, W.O. Bean, also joined briefly in the gunfight, shooting at and fortunately missing the fleeing engineer. "Jackson" returned the fire four times, advancing toward the two shadowy figures. One report said that Rube leaned out of the express car and got off a few shots himself, perhaps only in the air. Chester Hughes was hit in the left shoulder, the right groin, and the pit of the stomach. Mortally wounded and bleeding profusely, he staggered back aboard the train, helped by Wilkerson, and fell into the arms of a newsboy uttering his last words, "Butch, I am done for." Passengers, especially women and children, were panicking, screaming and clinging to each other.

When the gunfire ceased, "Jackson" returned to the express car as Rube was leaping to the ground. Neither of them was aware that anyone had been shot, and the African-American fireman hiding under the baggage car was assured by the bandits that no one was going to shoot him. The two then took their loot, $1500 in currency and $365 in silver, and returned to their horses nearby and quickly rode off. The engineer, satisfied the bandits were gone, gathered steam and moved the train up the track through the rain storm to Grenada, the telegraph lines having been cut between there and Duck Hill. Once alerted from Grenada, a special train provided by the Illinois Central brought Southern Express Superintendent George W. Agee, Memphis Police Captain George O'Haver, and Pinkerton Detective Burns to Duck Hill, also bringing stenographers to record the testimony of witnesses. Now murder had been added as a complication, energizing the authorities to find whoever was responsible.[231]

One unfortunate incident accruing from the robbery was a comment in the *Memphis Appeal* that Duck Hill was the home of a "regular gang living at or near Duck Hill . . . generally known and befriended by their neighbors." This led to an angry resolution by Duck Hill citizens calling the author of the article a "slanderous liar," and that the comment was a "lie blacker than the days of hell," casting a "hellish stain" on the good name of Duck Hill. The *Appeal* defended itself, surprised at the reaction from a community for which it "has never had anything but the kindest words of commendation and good will."[232]

Of course, the most immediate question was the identity of the robbers. Captain O'Haver was of the opinion that one of the men was Eugene Bunch, another wanted train robber, who bore a similar description as that of Rube Burrow.[233] Only weeks before, on November 3, the southbound New Orleans and Northeastern Railway had been robbed single-handedly by Bunch between Derby, Mississippi, and New Orleans. The New Orleans police quickly determined that Bunch was the culprit, arresting his girl friend and another cohort, but Bunch eluded capture and disappeared.[234] The similarities in the robberies and physical descriptions were sufficient to lead the Pinkertons to focus on finding Bunch, not Rube Burrow.[235] But impatient at the lack of progress by the Pinkertons since the Genoa robbery, the Southern Express Company launched its own fleet of detectives to take over the investigations and ferret out Burrow.

In the meantime, Rube and Leonard Brock rode through the rainstorm, crossing swollen rivers and streams, negotiating swamps, and stopping periodically to rest and to get something to eat where they could, primarily from African-Americans located in isolated cabins along the way. After following a circuitous route to throw off any pursuers, they finally arrived back at Vernon around midnight, five days later, on Thursday, December 20, staying at Jim Cash's place. After getting something to eat and feeding their horses, they moved into the woods about five miles off and set up camp. Nothing was mentioned to family members about the robbery, and they turned their horses over to John Thomas Burrow, Rube's brother, to sell for them. The two outlaws alternated staying at John Burrow's and Jim Cash's house at night, hiding in the woods during the daytime.[236]

The detectives of the Southern Express Company focused on tracking down Burrow, not believing that Eugene Bunch was responsible for the Duck Hill Robbery. In their view, the relatives of Burrow, whether of direct kin or an in-law, "were of a thriftless, restive spirit, and among them were many shrewd and cunning natures, who became the paid scouts of the outlaws."[237] It was felt that the best opportunity to nab Burrow was to watch members of his family and neighbors in the Lamar County countryside, in the hopes that they would slip up and reveal his whereabouts. Detectives swarmed through the county, one detective posing as a peddler with a rickety wagon containing clothing, even allegedly spending a night with Allen Burrow in April 1889 and selling a pair of trousers to Jim Cash.[238] But whether disguised as book agents, lightning rod salesmen, tinware peddlers, or even tramps, the people of Lamar County knew a detective when they saw one, buying little and talking even less, whether out of loyalty or fear.[239]

In Dallas, Texas, in early February 1889, Henderson Brumley went on trial in federal court for the June 1887 Benbrook robbery. The key witness was Bill Brock, who testified thoroughly as to how the robbery occurred and Brumley's prominent part in it. He told the jury that he had not been promised anything for his testimony. The defense, however, presented an array of witnesses who testified they had seen Brumley in and around Alexander at the time of the robbery, making it impossible for him to be in Tarrant County robbing trains. One witness, A.F. Harris, was the person Brock testified had provided dinner to the four robbers, including Brumley, on their return to Erath County from Benbrook. Harris testified that, indeed, he had provided four men a meal, but he had known Henderson Brumley for more than ten years and Brumley was not one of the four men. Also in evidence was a promissory note executed in Stephenville and dated the day of the robbery, which included Brumley's signature.[240] On February 6, the jury disregarded Brock's testimony and acquitted Brumley, perhaps because of an innate dislike for a "stool pigeon."[241] However, Brumley still had other charges pending and, given Brock's testimony and that of Askey, who also turned state's evidence, the prosecution wasn't going to give up.

In March, Brumley again went on trial in the federal court at Graham, this time for the Gordon robbery and the conspiracy to kidnap charge. In these trials, instead of Brock, Harrison Askey was the primary witness, but the defense attacked his credibility, as they had Brock's, this time by emphasizing the inconsistency in stories he gave about his alleged kidnapping. After a two-day trial "before a great number of spectators" on March 21 and 22, the result was the same—acquittal in both cases.[242]

United States Marshal Cabell received Bill Brock from Arkansas prison officials, Brock now having been pardoned by the Arkansas governor for the Genoa robbery as requested. He was transported to Dallas to be tried in federal court for the June 1888 Benbrook robbery.[243] In return for the pardon, Charles Pearre had promised the Arkansas governor to prosecute Brock to the fullest for his Texas crimes. However, on May 28, 1889, when the federal court refused to let Brock's testimony in the Brumley cases go before the jury, the sole evidence that the prosecution had to connect him with the Benbrook robbery, the jury was directed to return a not guilty verdict.[244] Bill Brock was a free man and ready to resume a new life with his family.

Rube Burrow and Leonard Brock remained secluded, hiding in the backwoods of Lamar County, never venturing far from home ground. In the early summer of 1889, Rube came up with an idea that he could be a more successful robber with a more effective disguise than a simple handkerchief across his face or burnt cork. He sent for a catalog from a firm in Chicago which advertised false beards and wigs. On receipt he perused the offerings and made his selection, sending five dollars on June 1 and ordering a beard four or five inches long and a wig, the color light red, "slightly grey," and "cropped hair." The letter was sent from the Jewell post office, which was in a small community near Vernon, but the return address was a poorly written "Sulligent," the town north of Vernon where the railroad came through. He signed the order with the name "W.W. Cain," who had been a minor official in Erath County.[245]

Because the word "Sulligent" was not legibly written on Rube's order, the Chicago firm sent the package containing the beard and wig to the Jewell post office. The postmaster there was Moses J. Graves, 41, married with five children as of 1880, who kept a small store along with the mail. Graves was familiar with the Burrow family, having advanced Rube's brother, John Thomas, $100 worth of livestock in March of 1888 to enable him to plant a crop, which John was to have repaid before November 1, 1888.[246]

Jim Cash, Rube's brother-in-law, called on Graves several times for the package. When the package finally arrived, it had been partially torn and the contents could be seen. According to Agee, when Cash again called for the package, which was addressed to "W.W. Cain," Graves told Cash that he could only turn it over to W.W. Cain, but having seen the contents he remarked that he was going to "take in the man that came for it and find what business he had with it." Agee concluded that Graves suspected it was intended for Burrow. Other accounts state that since Graves did not know a W.W. Cain, he returned the package to the merchant in Chicago after having seen the contents, which he supposedly told Cash when the package was called for. Yet another account claimed that Graves showed the open package to a crowd, some of whom even tried on the beard.

Cash relayed the message back to Rube, who reportedly became enraged and swore to get the package himself and kill anyone who stood in his way. He asked his partner, Leonard Brock, to go for it, but Brock refused, concerned that "if Graves was going to do a thing of that kind, [it] would stir up a big fuss." Before daylight on Tuesday, July 16, 1889, determined to get the package and the contents that he had paid for, Rube left Cash's home for Jewell. Deciding to wait until that evening, he loitered in the area until sundown, at which time he went into the postoffice to confront Graves, Agee describing Burrow and Graves as "companions and playmates in their boyhood."

Finding Graves and a young woman behind the store counter, Rube asked if he had any mail for W.W. Cain. Rube later told Brock that Graves made no response, but walked slowly toward a double-barreled shotgun leaning behind the counter. Rube asked a second time and Graves responded, "yes," but, according to Rube, kept moving toward the shotgun. The outlaw told him to get the mail, but when Graves grew closer to the shotgun, Rube drew his pistol and shot him, saying, "Get it for me or I will shoot you again." Rube later told Brock that Graves started to fall, and the lady behind the counter urged Rube not to shoot him again, volunteering to get the package for him, which she did. Rube took the package and left.

According to Agee's version, Graves responded that he did have the package, but couldn't give it to him. Rube then was supposed to have immediately drawn his sixshooter and shot the postmaster through the stomach, saying "I'll teach you to open my mail." In this account, Graves staggered and collapsed in a chair, gasping, "Rube Burrow, you have killed me." Rube pointed his revolver at the young girl assistant and ordered her to get his mail or he would blow her head off. Graves pointed it out for her and she retrieved the package for Burrow, then the outlaw left. Graves' wife rushed in to comfort her mortally wounded husband, according to Agee, and, before he expired, he made a statement before witnesses that it was indeed Rube Burrow who shot him.[247]

Upon Rube's return that evening, he and Brock retreated to the hills about a mile north of Jim Cash's place where they spent the night. Cash and John Thomas Burrow rode out in a wagon to see them, and they moved their camp nearer Cash's house, where John brought them something to eat.[248] Up to this point in his criminal career, Rube Burrow had not received much notice in the press. But the cold-blooded murder of Moses Graves turned him into a national figure. Stories of the killing and its aftermath were carried by the *New York Sun*, the *New York Tribune*, the *Boston Daily Globe*, and other newspapers of wide circulation. Fillmore Pennington, now the former sheriff of Lamar County, took a posse into the Burrow neighborhood in an attempt to locate the murderer, but returned without success.[249]

With the community vehemently outraged over Graves' killing, Lamar County Sheriff Lee S. Metcalfe arrested Allen Burrow, his son John Thomas Burrow, and Jim Cash, searching their homes and jailing them in Vernon on Friday, July 26, for harboring Rube and being accomplices in the murder of Graves. A posse of seventy-five men stood guard against any would-be vigilantes who might try to lynch them. That evening, the sheriff and a number of citizens, accompanied by ten detectives, scoured the areas where they thought Rube might be located.[250] It was later reported that detectives caught a fifteen-year-old son of John Thomas Burrow and threatened to hang him, throwing a noose over a limb, if he didn't tell what he knew about his uncle. With the rope tightened around his neck, the frightened boy told them, according to the report, that Rube and Brock had stayed with the boy's father for a month.[251]

Rewards totaling $6,000 for Rube's capture were now outstanding, and he was pictured as "defying the whole civil and military power of the State of Alabama, as well as scores of detectives employed by express and railroad companies."[252] On Sunday evening, when Lamar County Judge of Probate W.A. Young returned to Vernon and learned there was a movement to organize a lynch mob, he advised Sheriff Metcalfe to telegraph Alabama Governor Thomas Seay for troops to prevent violence and bloodshed. There was also concern that Rube and his "gang" might try a rescue attempt.

Governor Seay immediately ordered the mustering of thirty-five members of a militia group, the Birmingham Rifles, which arrived by train at Sulligent, the nearest railroad and telegraph station to Vernon, before noon on Tuesday, July 30. The soldiers were promptly ferried to Vernon by a convoy of wagons and posted around the jail.[253] Headed up by Birmingham's city attorney, Captain S.D. Weakley, the militia group was welcomed by the community for quieting the threat of violence that had been fomenting.[254]

Rube was reputed by the national press to be in hiding in the wild countryside only a few miles from Vernon, aided and abetted by an alleged army of well-armed desperadoes only willing to swoop down and rescue the prisoners. Rube was supposed to have sent Sheriff Metcalfe a message to "release them or expect dire penalties." In addition, a rumor spread that Jim Burrow, instead of being dead, had escaped from Arkansas and was on his way back to Alabama to help out his family.[255] To that report, Dr. G.M. Cantrell, the physician for the Arkansas penitentiary, and a prison hospital steward, assured the public that Jim was indeed dead and that when the body was put in its coffin, "life was certainly extinct."[256]

A hearing was held before Judge Young in a packed, suffocating courtroom in Vernon on Wednesday, July 31. A cousin of Moses Graves testified that she witnessed the shooting and heard her cousin say, "Rube Burrow, you can kill me, but I know you." Another witness stated that he had followed tracks from the post office to Jim Cash's home. There being no defense witnesses offered, the judge found there was no evidence linking Allen and John Thomas Burrow with the death of Graves and ordered them released. However, there was some "slight testimony" incriminating Jim Cash and a $1,000 bond was set for him. Some "substantial men" of the community stepped forward as bondsmen. That afternoon, the militia company left to return to Birmingham, the emergency now believed to be abated.

Two public meetings were held in Vernon the same day, each group passing resolutions "in regard to protecting the people from lawlessness and violence" through law and order rather than the establishment of mobs.[257] Ominously, however, one disgruntled vigilance group adopted resolutions stating:

> Certain parties of our county have been aiding and concealing criminals and outlaws contrary to law and to the injury of the fair name of the county. These parties are warned that as the peace and safety of the good people of the community is endangered by their actions, they must cease at once to conceal outlaws, or leave the county. They are further warned that if any other acts of violence occur, they will be held responsible and will meet swift and terrible punishment.[258]

Another group saw the murder of Graves by Rube Burrow as a "deplorable evil," warning that a "vigilant watch" would be maintained on those that would aid and abet Burrow, but that lawful methods would be pursued in the event that lawless acts continue to occur.[259] In an edition of the local newspaper, the *Vernon Courier*, a very articulate anonymous letter, signed by "one of the boys," assured the community that there were no hard feelings about the arrests and hearing, confident that it was the end of the matter as far as Allen Burrow, John Thomas Burrow, and Jim Cash were involved.[260] As it turned out, the Lamar County Grand Jury opted not to indict Jim Cash as an accessory to the murder of Moses Graves.[261]

Perhaps due to the sudden national notoriety of Rube Burrow, John Wanamaker, the United States Postmaster-General, announced on August 29 that it was rescinding a $200 reward offered the past July, replacing it with a $1,000 reward for the arrest and conviction of any person "making an armed attack upon any stage coach or railway train having mails in transit." This reward was to be offered through June 30, 1890.[262]

During all of the excitement, Rube and Leonard Brock remained hidden in the back country, food being brought to them by women of the Burrow family. After the release of the three, the two fugitives continued to camp out in the woods, Jim Cash now bringing them food. Rube refused to enter any house belonging to his kin, stating, "I might as well give myself up."[263] And for good reason: Southern Express detectives were still stealthily scouring the countryside, trying to get a fix on his whereabouts. With the murder of Graves, it was apparent that Rube had come home to Lamar County. But the detectives were thwarted at every turn by those committed to preventing the capture of the outlaws, the threat of vigilante action notwithstanding.

Around the first of September, as Rube and Leonard Brock decided to leave Lamar County, Rube's mother brought him a message from Rube Smith, 23, who wanted to see him. Smith, a first cousin of Rube's, lived in Crews, a few miles east of Sulligent, with his father and mother, James and Nancy Smith.[264] Reuben Smith, currently under indictment along with James McClung and an uncle, James Barker, for the robbery and beating of a farmer named Johnson, bore a bad reputation in the local community. He worked odd jobs to sustain himself, although he had at one time been an itinerant photographer. Standing just over five feet eight inches, Smith had an unusually low hairline across his forehead with deep-set blue eyes and dark brown hair.[265] Burrow had not seen his cousin since they were boys, and, leery that this may be a trap planned by detectives, he mulled it over for a few days. He finally sent his sister to tell Smith to meet him at the graveyard outside the Fellowship Church, about four miles from Vernon.[266]

Rube and Brock went to the cemetery well in advance of the time agreed on for Smith to be there, hiding in the bushes to see who would show up. Brock fell asleep while Rube remained vigilant. Rube grew tired of waiting, but as he was waking Brock to leave, they heard someone walking in the small graveyard. Rube watched for a few minutes, then greeted Smith and brought him over to introduce him to Brock, although not giving out his name. The three of them went to their camp near Cash's house, removing the next evening to near Smith's house, where they got food to eat. Burrow broached the idea of a train robbery, and Smith was agreeable, reassured by Burrow's record of successes.[267]

Likely passing along his train robbing methods to his new companion, Rube led his party through Buckatunna [buck-uh-ton-uh], Mississippi, about ten to twelve miles southeast of Waynesboro, then west to Ellisville, Mississippi, southwest of Waynesboro on the Northeastern Railway line, the Queen and Crescent Railway being his next intended target. However, once there, Rube decided that they would not get much money on that train, believing that shipments of money on that line were divided up among multiple trains. He determined to return to Buckatunna and take the Mobile and Ohio train there, hoping for a bigger haul since there was only a single daily express. The three trudged back the sixty miles from Ellisville, and camped out Sunday night, September 22, and the next night in an abandoned log cabin belonging to African-American Neil McAllister, some three miles from the Buckatunna station. They visited a trestle two miles south of the station as a likely stopping point. While they were waiting, Brock had some bread cooked at a white man's house, sending Smith after it. On Tuesday, September 24, Brock went into Buckatunna, purchased some meat, and took it back to their camp. Going to the trestle, they waited until the northbound train had gone through, readying themselves to take the southbound train.[268]

Chapter Five

"Don't Shoot Me Again."

Reuben Burrow as a young man. Alabama Department of Archives and History.

Southern Express Company Detective Thomas V. Jackson. George Agee.
Rube Burrow: King of Outlaws. Chicago: The Henneberry Co., 1890.

Shortly after three a.m., Wednesday, September 25, 1889, the southbound Mobile and Ohio passenger and mail train stopped briefly at the small Buckatunna station. As the train began steaming out of the station into the darkness, Engineer Jack Therrill heard a voice behind him in the cab. Thinking it was the fireman, he turned to be confronted by two men with pistols, Rube Burrow and Rube Smith. Leonard Brock waited at the trestle two miles south of the station. "Pull on out!" ordered Burrow, then added, "Don't be uneasy." Therrill assured him that he was not uneasy. In a menacing tone, Burrow threatened, "I am going to rob this train or kill every man on it." He directed the engineer to stop the train so that, just as in past robberies, the passenger cars would be straddling the trestle so that passengers could not safely get off.

The train stopped as directed where Brock was waiting, and the robbers had the engineer and fireman step to the ground. Brock walked to the express car, whose wooden door was open but access blocked by a locked iron grated door. Burrow and Smith and their prisoners followed. On the way, Burrow commented that he had decided to rob the train because there had been a boast in the newspapers during the spring that he couldn't rob it. Burrow directed the engineer to call out to the express messenger, J.W. Dunning, who was sitting on the far side of the car with his back toward them. Dunning turned, found three pistols pointed at him, and immediately unlocked the grated door. Conductor Billy Scholes jumped to the ground from the rear of the train carrying a Winchester rifle. Walking toward the group waving his lantern, he called out across the trestle, "What's the matter?" Burrow fired a shot over the engineer's head, calling out, "Come up here and you'll see what's the matter!" Therrill urged the robbers not to shoot any more as trainmen might open up with their weapons and shoot the engineer and fireman. Scholes retreated back to the train.

Burrow instructed Dunning to give him a hand and help him up into the car, warning him to handle his hand carefully, "as there are corns on it." Burrow had only been in the express car five or six minutes when Conductor Scholes again called out to know what was the matter, apparently unsure of what previously being shot at meant. Brock muttered, "Look out, I will settle him," walking forward a few paces, then calling out "Come and see." He squatted and fired a shot, then ran forward another ten feet or so and laid down flat on his stomach with his pistol at the ready. Burrow ordered Dunning out of the express car and had him hold the sack containing the $2,685 in loot until he reached the ground.

Burrow then ordered Therrill to move the train until the mail car cleared the trestle. Therrill told him that it was already clear, and, anyway, he probably didn't have enough steam built up to move the train at all. Burrow and Smith escorted Therrill and the fireman back to the engine where the fireman was ordered to get the fire started, Smith standing guard over him. Threatening to kill the fireman if he started up the train, Brock and Burrow then took Engineer Therrill to the mail car. Therrill was ordered aboard the mail car ahead of Burrow, who accused S.W. Bell, the postal agent, of trying to hide the registered packages. Bell denied it, saying that he had only turned his light down. He pointed out the registered mail, cautioning the robber that interfering with the mail would get the United States government down on them, to which Burrow responded, "That don't make any difference; I will take them anyhow." Burrow handed the packages, which contained $795, to Smith when he left the car, telling Bell to shut the door and keep it shut until the train left. Therrill was ordered to get back on the engine and move it out. It took about ten minutes for the engineer to get sufficient steam up. Burrow in cavalier fashion told him, "Hurry up to State Line [a station several miles south on the Alabama-Mississippi state line] and send a message up and down the road, so they can get after us. Tell the operator I say to hurry up about it. Tell the boss of those express cars to put steps on them, or I will stop robbing them. Don't ring the bell or blow the whistle, or I will shoot into the engine."

Brock and Smith melted into the woods next to the train, and as Burrow retreated to follow them, he called out, "Holler to those boys on the other side, and tell them to get back from the train," in an attempt to convince Therrill that they had a larger gang. Delayed thirty minutes, the train finally got underway and resumed its journey.[269]

The train went on down to Citronelle, Alabama, where an engine and train was provided to ferry a posse back to the scene of the crime.[270] The Mobile and Ohio immediately offered a $1,000 reward for the arrest of the robbers, publicly suspected to be Rube Burrow and his gang.[271] J.C. Clarke, the president of the railroad, ordered in dogs "trained to running men" to supplement the efforts of Superintendent

Agee of the Southern Express Company, who was also on the ground at the scene. Clarke wrote a postal inspector:

> We think that the Post Office Department ought to spare no expense to try to capture these depredators of the United States mails, as the General Government can command an unlimited number of detectives. If necessary one hundred (100) detectives should be put in the field in Alabama and Mississippi: prompt and speedy action is advisable. If the Department cannot put the detectives in the field, then it should offer a reward of $5,000 for the arrest and conviction of the robbers, and a proportionate amount for their arrest.[272]

Unfortunately, heavy rains continued, obliterating the trail for both the detectives and the dogs.[273] The three robbers stuck together until reaching Demopolis, Alabama, then split up, Rube Smith taking a train back to Lamar County and Burrow and Brock making their way back by foot, taking their time and carefully avoiding public roads, finally arriving by October 23, almost a month later.[274] Investigators scattered throughout southern Mississippi and Alabama looking for the robbers.

The expenses incurred in tracking the outlaws was a real concern of the railroad and express companies, leading them to look to the government to pick up the cost. Agee pointed out to the postal authorities that, in his opinion, the train robbers were not going to be caught with posses or "armed forces" scouring the countryside. "They can only be taken by the operation of skilled detectives detailed for the purpose, who will operate in the country to which we feel certain they will go, if they have not already done so, and by watching the mail, which may be sent by them to their relatives, or vice versa." Agee suggested that the Post Office employ a skilled detective to work with the Southern Express Company's detectives. With respect to the expense, Agee proposed that the costs be equitably split between the railroad, the express company, and the Post Office, which cost should not be more than $250 or $300 per month. The Post Office agreed to pay one-half the cost of printing reward circulars.[275]

Detectives were swarming all over Lamar County by the time Burrow and Brock got back. For about two weeks the two outlaws hid in the woods, staying at nights in Allen Burrow's hayloft, one sleeping while the other stood guard.[276] But an episode occurred at this point that inadvertently focused even more unwanted attention to Burrow.

On Thursday, October 24, in north central Alabama, Blount County Sheriff A.H. Morris received information that two men, believed to be Rube Burrow and a companion, were then at the house of a man named Bud Ashworth near Brooksville. The sheriff's brother, J.E. Morris, who was also his chief deputy, rounded up five men and went to Ashworth's cabin. Spreading out before the cabin's only door, the posse called on "Rube" to come out and give himself up. The two men inside grabbed one of the women of the household and presented themselves at the door with her as a shield, one of the men leveling a Winchester at the posse and declaring he would die before surrendering. The two men made their way with their hostage to some nearby woods, then, releasing her and firing at the lawmen, scampered into the undergrowth.[277]

The sheriff immediately called on citizens to join the posse and a major manhunt was undertaken. On Friday, two of the sheriff's men, Henry Anderton (or Anderson) and Penn Woodward, were killed and a third, John Hearn (or Herring), was badly wounded by the two fleeing men. One of the pursuing dogs was shot to death by the men on Sunday. By Monday morning, October 28, armed citizens scouring the countryside had been joined by Southern Express detectives, including Superintendent George Agee and two bloodhounds.

About five miles from the Ashworth cabin, at Sand Mountain, the two men were spotted and a gunfight broke out for several hours, resulting only in another bloodhound being killed. The men being pursued were sharp marksmen, and their pursuers learned quickly to keep their heads down. That afternoon, some twenty-five special officers from Birmingham, sent by the chief of the police at the request of Governor Seay, arrived to join in the hunt. Once more the two men escaped into the woods and the pursuit was finally halted by Sheriff Morris and the detectives. The press now assumed that the two men were Rube Burrow and "Joe Jackson."[278] As it turned out, the two men were actually moonshiners named Charlie Smith, who also used the alias of Johnson, and his companion, Jim Stringer.[279] But Rube's notoriety had now become national, as major newspapers vied with one another to tell the most lurid tales. He and "Joe Jackson" continued to be portrayed as the two Blount County fugitives.

On Thursday, October 31, E.W. Barrett, a reporter for the *Atlanta Constitution*, ventured into Lamar County to visit Allen Burrow for an interview.[280] The reporter also talked with Jim Cash, who claimed that when he went to Jewel, he asked for any mail for W.H. Cash, his brother, not W.W. Cain, and Postmaster Graves must have heard him wrong. Cash said that Rube was getting tired of the outlaw life. "I believe if the governors of the different states that have offered rewards for him, and the railroads and express companies would agree to pardon him if he would settle down and live honestly in some place, he would give himself up and do it." He added, "They've got to kill him before he sees them, or they'll never get him." Allen Burrow, commiserating over what a good boy he had raised, pleaded that Rube didn't kill Graves: "Graves never saw Rube in his life and couldn't have known him." However, he was able to chuckle about the swarms of detectives who flooded the county looking for Rube. He pointed out a nearby hickory tree and commented about all the lawmen who continuously camped out behind that tree watching his place. Rube's son William was described by his grandfather as a "chunky little fellow of twelve." A neighbor told the reporter that the boy was anxious to grow up and join his father in holding up trains.[281]

On the following Sunday, November 3, complete with illustrations, the *Constitution* printed a multiple column story, headlined "Red Rube! Burrow and His Bloody Career in the Southwest." Now began the myth-making. Rube was described as "the most reckless and daring outlaw and train robber this country has ever produced . . . His record of lawlessness has not been equaled by the noted Jesse James."[282] Not to be outdone, on November 6 the *New York Sun* itself ran a multiple-column story, liberally borrowing from the *Constitution*, labeling Rube Burrow as the "King of Outlaws," who bid defiance to all pursuers in a criminal career that "eclipses Jesse James's accomplishments." Another newspaper, however, the *New York Daily Tribune*, took exception to the lurid accounts being written about Rube Burrow, i.e., that he was a "whole feud and a sheriff's posse thrown in." To a far-fetched allegation that Burrow was going to write a book about his career as a road agent, the *Tribune* observed that the nearest approach Rube ever made to literary accomplishment had been to "wad his shotgun with the local paper."[283]

Barrett also sought an interview with Rube himself, offering $200, but Rube decided against a meeting, concerned that a more complete description of him would only serve to help the detectives looking for him. [284] It was reported that Barrett went to the Burrow house a few days after the *Constitution* article appeared, and that he had subsequently disappeared.[285] As it turned out, Mr. Barrett was okay, and on Sunday, November 10, the *Constitution* printed a purported interview with the wanted man, a total piece of fiction to generate sales of the newspaper.[286] The article, which was based on events published in past accounts of Burrow, sought to portray him as a cavalier bandit, inspired by the exploits of Jesse James, who initially joined Nep Thornton's gang in Texas. To help perpetuate the Robin Hood myth being created, Barrett quoted "Burrow": "I have held up trains, and I have killed a few men because I had to, but I never robbed a poor man in my life, and I'm never going to."[287]

Lauding Barrett for his "brave venture" into Burrow country, the *Constitution* sent 9,000 copies of its November 10 edition containing the "interview" by special train early in the morning to Birmingham in order to scoop the *Birmingham Age-Herald*. But the *Age-Herald* had heard about the story in advance and on the same day published an article mocking Barrett and proclaiming his interview with Rube as "pure Buncombe," likewise sending thousands of copies to be hawked by newsboys in Atlanta. It was claimed that a former Lamar County deputy sheriff had been paid ten dollars a minute to pose as Burrow for a twenty-minute interview by Barrett. The two newspapers bantered back and forth for several days thereafter trying to one-up each other, although the *Constitution* never admitted that the interview was a hoax.[288] The *Vernon Courier* in Lamar County lamented that all of the sensational stories being irresponsibly published by the media about Rube Burrow could only do "great harm . . . as long as young boys are allowed to read such stuff," thus kindling criminal thoughts and inspiring copycat crimes.[289]

All the while the search for Rube and his associates was continuing. The detectives were fairly sure about the participation of Rube Burrow and "Joe Jackson" in the Buckatunna robbery, but were puzzled about who the third man was. A new Southern Express detective now brought into the pursuit was Thomas V. Jackson. Born about 1854 in Mississippi and just under six feet tall with a neat brown

Rick Miller

moustache, the stocky, jovial detective enjoyed a good cigar.[290] When Rube Smith returned to Lamar County, flashing and spending more money than a man of his limited means was ever likely to possess, word got back to Detective Jackson, who surmised that Smith might be the third member of the gang.

Rube Smith was hiding near his father's home while Jackson was searching for him. In the latter part of November, an old acquaintance of Smith's, Jim McClung, 22, returned from a trip to the Indian Territory, to visit relatives in Itawamba County, in the northeastern part of Mississippi, thirteen miles from Tupelo. He ran across his old friend Smith, who told him that Rube Burrow, the noted train robber, was in the area, introducing him to a man who claimed to be Burrow. The three agreed to go to Alabama to pull a hold-up, and McClung and Smith took a train to Crews Station, near where Smith's father lived in Lamar County, and where they were met by "Burrow" on Monday, December 7. The three plotted to hold up a train two miles north of the small town of Amory, Mississippi, just northwest across the state line a few miles from Sulligent, Alabama. At the time agreed on, they met, but the trio got cold feet and abandoned the robbery plan. They hung around Amory for several days visiting the saloons, and "Burrow" told the two to meet him at Smith's house in Lamar County. Smith and McClung went to the Amory depot station on Friday, December 13, to take the train to Sulligent.[291]

At about eleven o'clock in the morning, Tom Jackson happened to walk into the Amory railroad station and spotted Rube Smith, with his distinctive low hairline, sitting with McClung in a rather chilly waiting room. Not willing to try an arrest by himself, the detective went outside to get the help of detective Thomas J. Aiken. Aiken went inside by himself and engaged the two in conversation, while Jackson sauntered back in and took a seat. The two fugitives decided to go into Amory and get a drink, and the two detectives accompanied them offering to buy a round. Smith and McClung refused the offer, and Jackson, still looking for the most opportune time to arrest them, began to criticize the railroad for not having a warm waiting room. The four soon returned to the railroad station. While the two outlaws were inside, Jackson dispatched Aiken to get a third detective, John Clay, in order to make an arrest.

When Clay arrived, Jackson and Aiken went into the waiting room, Aiken pulling a pistol to cover McClung while Jackson drew down on Smith. McClung, caught off guard, gave up his pistol and surrendered peacefully. Smith raised his hands, but demanded that Jackson show his authority. When Jackson reached for Smith's pistol, which was strapped to his shoulder, Smith also went for it. The two struggled around the waiting room, Jackson hitting him sharply on the head with his pistol. Aiken rushed over and also hit Smith across the head with his pistol. Smith grabbed at Jackson's pistol, pressing it against the detective's stomach, and tried to pull the trigger. Jackson ruthlessly wrenched the pistol away, at which time it discharged, the bullet piercing McClung's hat and taking off a small piece of his scalp. The terrified McClung hollered, "don't shoot me again." The struggle with Smith was carried out to the gallery of the station where the outlaw was finally disarmed, at which time he surrendered. The two prisoners were immediately transported to Jackson's home town, Aberdeen, Mississippi.[292] Smith was then taken to stand charges at Waynesboro in Wayne County, Mississippi, the county in which was located Buckatunna.[293]

On Tuesday, December 17, Rube Smith was in state court at Waynesboro for a preliminary examination of the robbery charge. Neil McAllister, the black man in whose cabin the robbers stayed at Buckatunna, identified Smith as having been in the area at the time of the robbery. In addition to Tom Jackson, Jim McClung also testified, telling about his relationship with Smith and what Smith told him about the Buckatunna robbery. After the testimony was heard, the court set a bond of $5,000 pending a grand jury determination, and Smith was sent to the jail at Meridian for safe keeping.[294] While in jail at Meridian, an escape plot by Smith was thwarted, he planning to overpower a jailer and flee with others.[295] The third man who posed as Burrow, though publicly unidentified, was known to Agee and his detectives, but because he only contemplated rather than committed train robbery, he was allowed to go free and go to the Indian Territory.[296] McClung continued to be held in jail at Waynesboro until April 1890, still suspected of being involved in the Buckatunna robbery, when the Blount County sheriff took him as a suspect in the shooting of the two deputies in that county the previous October.[297]

Lamar County continued to be infested with detectives, all looking for Rube Burrow. Close watch was maintained on the homes of Allen Burrow, John Thomas Burrow, and Jim Cash. All manner of disguises were resorted to: itinerant peddlers, lightning rod salesmen, tramps begging from house to house, etc.[298] One detective, George Roberts, not being too quiet locally about his hunt for Burrow, was sidetracked and arrested when he was found in possession of jewelry taken in a store burglary in Vernon.[299] A legitimate peddler of Bibles was physically run out of Lamar County by armed men who had stopped him and found in his pocket a written description of Burrow.[300]

It was obvious that the heat of pursuit was making Rube's stay on his home grounds more and more unfeasible and, with winter coming on, his father suggested that he look for a new sanctuary. On November 20, after hiding out in Lamar County for about a month, both at his father's place and near Jim Cash, Rube and Leonard Brock trekked on foot to near Columbus, Mississippi, southwest of Vernon across the state line, when the determination was made that they ought to go to Florida. The law would not think of looking for the fugitives there. Brock, not possessing the physical robustness of his companion, quickly suggested that they return to Lamar County, buy some horses, and ride rather than walk to Florida as Rube proposed. But Rube was concerned that their trail would be too obvious to the detectives. He suggested as an alternative that they go back to Jim Cash's place, buy his wagon and yoke of oxen, and go to Florida in that manner, disguised as laborers. Brock didn't care for the idea, but Rube was persuasive and they returned to Vernon and arranged the sale with Cash through Allen Burrow. The father returned Rube and Brock to Columbus hidden in a covered wagon, while Cash followed with the wagon and two oxen, which Rube dubbed "Mack" and "Brandy." The four rendezvoused in Columbus on November 28. Provisions were purchased and stored in the wagon and, at ten o'clock that evening, the two fugitives started their southward journey, while Allen Burrow and Cash returned to Lamar County announcing that the wagon and oxen had been sold.[301]

It didn't take long for the detectives flooding the county and watching friends and relatives of Rube Burrow to figure out that the outlaw and "Joe Jackson" had fled the area. Tom Jackson was not satisfied with Jim Cash's story that he had sold his oxen team, and since there was no corroboration of the sale, decided that the detectives had to locate the oxen and wagon because of the likelihood that Rube was involved. In the meantime, Rube and Brock arrived with the team on December 14 at Flomaton, Alabama, a small station on the Louisville and Nashville Railroad in Escambia County, sitting directly on Alabama's southern border with the Florida Panhandle. At this point, although the two had made inquiries about logging jobs in Santa Rosa County, Florida, across from Flomaton, Brock had second thoughts about going into Florida. He left Burrow at Flomaton, headed for Pleasant Hill in Sabine Parish, Louisiana, intending to stay with an uncle, J.T. Harrell, but telling Rube that he had cattle business in Texas. The plan was for him to meet Rube on February 20, 1890, at Dyers Station, a few miles east of Mobile, with a view to robbing the Louisville and Nashville train there.[302]

On the morning of December 15, calling himself by the name of Ward, Rube Burrow took his ox team on the ferry across the Escambia River into Santa Rosa County. The county was wild and unsettled, consisting of dense canebrakes and swamps and lagoons. The Blackwater and Yellow Rivers meandered through the county, emptying into the Gulf of Mexico. Much of the county was best described as inaccessible marshland.[303] Two weeks before Christmas, Rube, still under the alias of Ward, took a job with W.B. Allen's logging company on Live Oak Creek, using his team to haul feed to Allen's camp from Broxson's (or Broxton's) Ferry on the Yellow River, ten miles south of Milton, Florida, and a distance of about eighteen miles from Allen's camp.[304] The loggers becoming acquainted with the recent arrival thought him likeable but somewhat mysterious, "Ward" choosing to remain close-mouthed about his past. Using the work as a justification for remaining secluded in the area, it was noted that "Ward" enjoyed going hunting often.[305]

Tom Jackson doggedly pursued any information as to Burrow's whereabouts. On January 15, 1890, he finally got lucky and found the trail of Burrow and Brock near Carrollton, Mississippi, some forty miles south of Columbus, evidently headed for southern Alabama or Florida. The detective guessed that the next spot to best pick up their trail was at Gainestown in the southwest section of Alabama where they might cross the Alabama River. Arriving there on January 24, he developed information that the two fugitives and the ox cart had indeed crossed the river on December 11. It did not take him long to learn of their presence in Flomaton.

On the 29th of January, Jackson learned where Burrow had taken the ferry across the Escambia River by himself, now concluding that "Joe Jackson" had separated from Burrow. The description given of the man with the oxen matched that of Rube Burrow.[306] When the detective reached Broxson's Ferry, he found no ferry there at the time, but he encountered a passerby and learned about the newcomer named Ward and his job of hauling feed. Jackson ascertained that Ward's routine was to leave the logging camp about seven a.m., reaching the ferry about two in the afternoon. After loading his wagon, he would spend the night at Broxson's nearby house, about a mile from the ferry, then make an early return to Allen's camp the next morning. Unable to cross the river at that time, Jackson returned to Milton, the county seat of Santa Rosa County, and sent a telegram in code to the authorities of the Southern Express Company: "I expect to secure title to tract number one, about ten miles south of here, Wednesday, February 6th. The papers are all in good shape." The term "number one" designated Rube Burrow, and the remainder of the wire gave the details for the date and place of attempted capture.[307]

At four in the morning on February 6, Jackson, accompanied by two detectives named Vincent and Shelton, along with three citizens from Milton, left in a hack for Broxson's Ferry, leaving the graded road and taking a rutted track through a swamp. They arrived at the ferry crossing about eleven a.m., finding Broxson and his son, Willie, there, as well as a small boat loaded with supplies that Rube was scheduled to pick up. Jackson had planned to cross the river and try to nab Burrow as he came down the road toward the ferry, but the presence of the loaded boat presented a better lure. Because the road on the other side of the river had sparse timber, it might be difficult to sufficiently hide from the outlaw's view. So Jackson and his men, all armed with shotguns, took up positions behind large fallen cypress trees and other foliage where they could watch the boat and waited.

Broxson had formed somewhat of a friendship with "Ward," who had charmed him and his family with his folksy anecdotes and stories. However, he had little choice but to cooperate with these detectives, no doubt somewhat shocked to learn the true identity of his frequent guest. Compelled to remain with the detectives, Broxson did convince

Jackson to let his son go home. Broxson was posted up the road to alert the detectives of Ward's approach. But by mid-afternoon, the outlaw had yet to make an appearance, although he had never before failed to appear before three p.m. At about five o'clock, a black logger from Allen's camp came by and told them that one of Ward's oxen had been sick and that Ward would probably not come until the next day. Not sure when the outlaw might actually come, however, the detectives remained in hiding until after darkness fell. Broxson later claimed that the detectives built a fire against the night chill and consumed a lot of whiskey to keep warm.

Figuring that if Burrow did show up, the outlaw would spend the night with Broxson and load the supplies the next morning, Jackson had his posse move up to an abandoned schoolhouse not far from the ferryman's house and keep watch the rest of the night. The driver of the hack from Milton was instructed not to follow them, but the order was not followed. Just as the detectives approached the schoolhouse, Burrow appeared, driving up to the Broxson gate and, not seeing the detectives in the darkness, inquired of Mrs. Broxson where her husband was. She told him that he had been down at the river all day with a party of hunters. Alerted reluctantly by Broxson to Burrow's arrival, the detectives quickly took cover behind available foliage. Burrow got his Marlin rifle from his wagon and started to walk down to the ferry to find Broxson. But he bristled when he heard strange voices and saw the hack. Maybe there had been something unusual in Mrs. Broxson's voice. Intuitively, he knew it was a trap and ran into the swampy forest, once more eluding his pursuers before they could spring their trap.

Jackson and his men, caught by surprise, could do nothing but stand guard over Burrow's wagon and oxen the remainder of the night in the vain hope that their quarry would return. However, Burrow returned to Allen's camp where he rounded up some provisions and left early Thursday morning, without collecting the wages owed him by Allen. On Friday, February 8, the detectives took the oxen and wagon back to Milton where it was sold for eighty dollars. The buyer promptly announced that he would put Burrow's team on exhibit at the upcoming Mardi Gras, and a newspaper article facetiously noted that the Southern Express Company was "over a cart and yoke of oxen and short a train robber."[308] On February 8, in Birmingham, Superintendent Agee had to publicly admit the failure to nab Burrow.[309]

While the rest of the posse returned to Milton, Jackson remained alone in the swamps, doggedly looking for the elusive bandit. Burrow fled further south into Santa Rosa County, finding refuge with a family around East Bay in the county's southernmost part, about four miles from the Gulf of Mexico. James H. Wells, an elderly and partially paralyzed man, lived there in a dilapidated cabin with his wife and four children,[310] and Burrow paid him for food. Agee characterized Wells as having an "unsavory reputation" in that area. Burrow stayed with the family through the spring and summer of 1890, perhaps because of the companionship of Wells' two daughters, for whom he was said to have played "the part of the gay Lothario."[311] It was said that the two girls brought him food and drink, for which the bandit handsomely compensated Wells. When there was no danger, a white flag was hoisted by the house on an old ox whip.[312]

On February 20, when Burrow failed to appear as scheduled at Dyers Station, east of Mobile, Leonard Brock waited one day, went to Mobile, then back to New Orleans. In mid-March, newspaper reports declared that Tom Jackson was missing and it was rumored falsely that a bullet-riddled body found in Lamar County was his.[313] In March of 1890, the former sheriff of Covington County, Alabama, John Penton, who was wanted for murder in Alabama and hiding in Florida, made an offer to catch Rube Burrow in return for clemency. Superintendent Agee pondered the offer, then suggested to Alabama Governor Thomas Seay that justice might best be served by employing one criminal to catch another. The governor, attuned to the political winds, declined, although recognizing Agee's "laudable zeal."[314]

In early April Rube Smith went on trial in state court at Waynesboro for the Buckatunna robbery. Witnesses, including Jim McClung, testified as to what Smith had told them about committing the robbery with Burrow. However, James Smith, Rube's father, testified that Rube was at home in Lamar County on the night of the robbery, as did his uncle, Jim Barker. For such testimony, Barker and James Smith were later indicted and tried for perjury. Rube Smith testified in his own defense, denying commission of the robbery, but was unable to explain how he had so much cash on him at the time of his arrest. The Lamar County sheriff stood by in the event of an acquittal, both Smith and McClung being wanted back home as suspects in the beating of a farmer named Johnson in January of 1889.[315] However, by the time the local court decided that McClung should be handed over to the sheriff, it was found that he had been spirited away by Agee and his men, likely because he might be needed as a witness in the event Smith's case was overturned on appeal.[316]

After eight hours of passionate argument by the lawyers on Friday evening, April 11, the jury quickly convicted Rube Smith the next morning and sentenced him to the maximum punishment of ten years imprisonment in the state penitentiary. The Wayne County District Attorney who prosecuted the case, J.H. Neville, did not feel that the sentence was sufficiently harsh, and urged Agee to contact federal authorities to prosecute Smith for the mail offenses, a federal violation. Agee wrote the postal inspector, reminding him of the $1,000 reward offered, suggesting that it be paid to Tom Jackson.[317] The postal authorities thought federal prosecution was a good idea and contacted the United States Attorney, who thought he could have an indictment returned by a federal grand jury in Jackson, Mississippi, in May.[318] In the meantime, only thirty days after being admitted to the Jackson penitentiary, Smith was discovered planning yet another escape, and he was immediately adorned with a heavy ball and chain.[319]

On May 6, 1890, Reuben Smith was indicted by a federal grand jury for mail robbery.[320] Three weeks later, on May 28, a jury was selected at Jackson and the mail robbery case was presented. However, two days later, after presentation of the evidence by United States Attorney Albert Lea, including the testimony of Jim McClung, the jury was unable to agree on a verdict and a mistrial was declared.[321] Perhaps, as with the Texas trial of Henderson Brumley, the jury was leery of a witness who might benefit from his testimony by virtue of a plea agreement. A new trial was reset for November, and McClung was ordered held as a material witness until that time.[322] Ascribing the mistrial to the quality of Smith's lawyers, George Agee suggested that the second trial add co-counsel in the person of Wayne County District Attorney John Neville.[323]

The hunt for Rube Burrow continued. A Southern Express Company detective, John A. Sullivan, was of the opinion that the outlaw was back in Lamar County, helped by friends and relatives, and spending his time, fishing, hunting, and working with a moonshine still.[324] On June 11, 1890, the St. Louis, Arkansas, and Texas Railroad was derailed and held up by robbers two miles south of Texarkana, Arkansas. A tramp stealing a ride was killed, and the messenger had his ear shot off for resisting. Of course, the robbery was immediately blamed on Rube Burrow and his gang, although Burrow continued to hide in Florida.[325]

Leonard Brock, alias "Joe Jackson," after failing to meet Burrow at Dyer station on February 20, understood that, in such event, the two were to meet in Lamar County around the first of September. Brock was aware from press reports that Burrow had escaped capture in Florida. From February, Brock meandered around the country, repeatedly returning to Mobile where he suffered a bout of measles. Throughout the spring he traveled across Mississippi, finally ending up at Allen Burrow's place in Lamar County around the first of May, where he slept in the barn. Mrs. Burrow came out and asked him for the whereabouts of her son, which he did not know. He then stayed hidden in the loft of the Burrow house until Tuesday, July 15. That evening he left the Burrow place on a mule and met Jim Cash, who loaned him twenty-five dollars and escorted him to the small village of Fernbank, south of Vernon. Brock handed over to him his pistol, apparently now remorseful about the criminal path in which he found himself caught up, vowing to never "use another pistol."[326]

Brock's intended destination was Columbus, Mississippi, then on to somewhere in Kentucky to start a new life.[327] Detective Tom Jackson, returned from Florida, was back in Lamar County and camping out at night near Allen Burrow's place. He saw the old man and Jim Cash repeatedly visiting each other and figured they were preparing for a trip. When Cash and Brock rode to Fernbank, the detectives, deeming it not safe to attempt an arrest on the open road, presumed that "Joe Jackson" intended to take a train on the Georgia Pacific. Detectives were placed on trains east and west of Fernbank, and Jackson himself boarded a train at Kennedy, east of Fernbank, along with ex-Lamar County Sheriff Pennington and current Lamar County Sheriff Lee Metcalfe. When their train stopped at Fernbank at 11:30 a.m., Wednesday, July 16, Brock, wearing a jeans suit and a derby hat, boarded the train and took a seat in the ladies' car. The lawmen remained in the smoking car, but kept an eye on him. At the next station, heading toward Columbus, Jackson took a seat in the ladies car immediately behind Brock, and sat there until the train reached Columbus. As Brock stepped off the car onto the station platform at Columbus, the detectives covered him with pistols and he surrendered without resistance.[328] Only Rube Burrow now remained at large.

Chapter Six

"I Surrender! I Surrender!"

*John McDuffie. George Agee, Rube Burrow: King of
Outlaws. Chicago: The Henneberry Co., 1890.*

Jefferson Davis "Dixie" Carter. George Agee, Rube Burrow:
King of Outlaws. Chicago: The Henneberry Co., 1890.

Rick Miller

When captured, Leonard Brock, alias "Joe Jackson," gave the detectives another alias name of John B. Winslow, denying any knowledge of Rube Burrow and train robbing. Two pistols and $100 in cash were recovered from his person. Agee accompanied the detectives in transporting Brock to Birmingham, where he was jailed until the authorities could figure out where he was to be taken for trial. Agee told the newspapers that "Joe Jackson" was the "brains of the gang," and that he would "rather have him a prisoner than Rube Burrows himself." Arrogantly, Brock asked for a receipt for his money and arms, ordered a lunch to be brought to him, and, after surveying his cell, offered to pay the jail turnkey if he would clean it up for him.[329]

Brock was taken on to Memphis, Tennessee, on July 17, where he was held and questioned for about an hour in George Agee's office on the third floor of the Southern Express Company's building. He was stripped and his body examined for identifying marks and scars. Brock alias Winslow was then taken to a cell at the local police station for safekeeping. While awaiting the arrival of persons who could positively identify "Joe Jackson," the detectives persistently continued to question him. He was soon satisfactorily identified,[330] and on Saturday, July 19, Brock finally relented and gave a detailed confession, including his true name, to Agee and Detective Tom Jackson.

According to Agee, the confession as to both the Duck Hill and Buckatunna robberies came as a result of Brock being "confronted with the overwhelming evidence against him."[331] The detectives threatened to prosecute him for the murder of Chester Hughes at Duck Hill, which involved a capital murder and would likely result in him being hanged. In return for his confession, they promised to prosecute him only for the robbery at Buckatunna, which carried a life sentence. Very real, also, was the likelihood that, if returned to Duck Hill, the outraged friends of Hughes might attempt to lynch him. In addition, he was told that members of the Burrow family had implicated him. Mulling all of this over, Brock initially maintained his silence, but when arrangements began to be made to transport him to Duck Hill, he weakened and gave a full statement of his and Burrow's movements. He even admitted that it was his pisol that likely killed Chester Hughes at Duck Hill. The only stipulation on which he insisted, which the authorities honored, was that his confession would not be made public while Rube Burrow was alive.[332]

When asked his opinion of Rube Burrow, Brock added to his statement:

> I have often heard him say that if the detectives crowded him that he would kill them, or he would shoot his way out if they did not kill him. He said it would be a life and death fight. I have heard him say more than once that if he could get a large lot of money he would leave enough at home to take care of his children, and then, if he could, would go off where he would not be bothered, and lead a quiet life.[333]

On Monday, July 21, Brock waived an examining trial before the United States Commissioner at Jackson, Mississippi, and, in default of $10,000 bond, was placed in the state penitentiary there the same day for safekeeping until the November term of the federal court.[334] It was feared that the county jail at Waynesboro was insufficiently secure to withstand a possible rescue attempt by Brock's criminal cohorts.[335] When Brock was taken inside the prison at Jackson, Rube Smith was working in a prison shop not far off. A Southern Express official accompanying Tom Jackson told Smith that "Joe Jackson" had been captured, but Smith quickly denied any knowledge of him, even when Brock was pointed out to him through a window. The detectives revealed to Smith a little information about his association with Burrow (no doubt gleaned from Brock), leading Smith to believe that perhaps the evidence against him was now stronger than at his trial in Waynesboro. As a result, he began searching for a way to make an escape.

Once settled in at his new quarters in the Jackson, Mississippi, penitentiary, awaiting trial, Leonard Brock, still using the name J.B. Winslow, wrote his uncle, J.T. Harrell, at Pleasant Hill, Louisiana, asking him to come see him in prison as he wanted him to sell some land he owned in Coffee County, Alabama, and turn the proceeds over to his mother. "I will not put my right name to this. I am sure you will know the writing anyhow." Harrell visited his nephew around September 1, learning for the first time of the accusations against him.[336]

Reuben Smith was also doing some writing, but for a different reason. He made contact with Jeff Moody, a fellow prisoner from

Itawamba County in northern Mississippi, near the Alabama state line, who was within days of being released. He cautiously sounded Moody out as to whether he could be trusted, then asked him to take some letters out to his father. On August 24, he gave three letters to Moody, all addressed to James Smith. Smith knew that James Cash would likely be a witness against him, and, after the Southern Express official had shared with him some of the new information about his association with Burrow, Smith realized that someone was giving the detectives information that could only be known to an insider. Smith asked his father to get him three pistols and twenty dollars, to be delivered by his uncle, Jim Barker, along with Moody, who he believed could be trusted and would know how to smuggle the pistols to him. The plan was for someone, likely Moody, to scale the prison walls and hide the pistols in a drawer of Smith's workbench. At six the next evening, when the bell sounded ending the work day and guards escorted the prisoners back to their cells, Smith planned to provide a weapon to Brock and another convict, then take guards prisoner until they were able to get out of the prison.[337]

> I no Just what I am talking about now, thay are goin to send me up salt creek if they can. this is all the chance for me & I no it & if you don't do something now I am going to give the gards a faire shot at me—if they kill me all rite & if they miss me all rite but if you will do what I want you to do theay wont bee eny Danger of geting hurt for i can make them turn me rite out without eny trouble.[338]

Unfortunately for Smith, Moody had no intention of helping him and had already revealed the plot to prison officials, who advised him to go along with the scheme. Smith's letters were handed over by Moody, and the prison authorities then turned them over to the Southern Express detectives as further evidence of Smith's guilt. Another escape plot foiled, Smith was placed in irons and isolated in a dungeon to await his retrial on federal charges.[339]

Rube Burrow remained hidden in the swamps of Santa Rosa County in the Florida panhandle. Tom Jackson had learned from Brock that he and Burrow had worked at the logging camp of John Barnes in the spring of 1888, where Rube had learned how to saw logs.

Jackson located Barnes near Castleberry in Conecuh County, Alabama, just north of the Florida state line. The detective deduced from Barnes' description of the man "Ward" who worked for him that it was Rube Burrow. Barnes, who was part Indian and a native of Santa Rosa County, agreed to help Jackson smoke out Burrow in country with which he was very familiar.

Around August 20, Barnes ventured into Santa Rosa County, making contact with James Wells, whom he knew well. He told the elderly man that he was thinking about moving back from Alabama. Wells, without solicitation, suggested that he might join in a partnership with "Ward." Barnes pretended to be somewhat reluctant about accepting the offer, then relented and agreed to the enterprise. Barnes stayed with Wells at his cabin until Rube sent word that he would meet with him on Sunday, August 31, somewhere in the area. With that information in hand, Barnes returned to his father's place in Alabama where Tom Jackson was waiting to hear from him. Jackson puzzled over why Rube would want such a delay in meeting with Barnes. However, Barnes returned at the scheduled time, only to be told by Wells that Burrow had declined the idea of the partnership and would not meet with him. In actuality, Rube was, of course, aware of the detectives searching for him throughout the county and reasonably suspected that this was another trap.[340] Rube had another enterprise in mind.

At 7:50 p.m., Monday, September 1, 1890, the northbound passenger train Number Six of the Louisville and Nashville Railroad left Mobile, headed northeast to Flomaton on the Alabama-Florida border. The train was supposed to make a connection with a train from Pensacola, but that train was delayed, throwing the L&N train off its schedule by twenty minutes. Once the connection was made and Engineer Robert Sizer was preparing to resume the train's journey, the porter spotted a man running alongside the train and climbing onto the train just as it started up. As it was not uncommon for another engineer or train man to share a ride in this manner to the next station, the porter did not think much of it. Climbing over the coal tender and peering down into the engine cab, the man, who was wearing a red bandana mask, produced two pistols and, with a threat that he would kill the engineer, ordered the train to go on to the Escambia River, about a mile to the north, and stop on the trestle. The fireman,

African-American John Duval, was ordered to move away from the furnace. The engineer obeyed the order and stopped the train when the bandit told him to stop. The engine and express car were across the trestle, while the passenger cars remained on the trestle and on the south side of the river, effectively preventing any interference by passengers.

The bandit handed a coal pick to Sizer and ordered the two train men to precede him to the express car. Duval, however, broke and ran. The bandit called out a threat and fired two shots at the fleeing fireman, missing his target. In the first class coach, train conductor John C. Elliott, wondering why the train had not picked up much speed after leaving Flomaton, was at even more of a loss when the train stopped. He stepped out on the coach platform in time to see the flash of the gunshots fired at Duval. Thinking tramps may have gotten into a fight with the engineer, all of a sudden a sharp warning came to him out of the darkness: "Take in your head!" The conductor immediately reentered the car, now fairly sure that a robbery was in progress.

Passengers had also grasped that idea and fled from the second class car and the smoking car into the first class car. Following the usual routine, a scramble to hide valuables commenced. Shoes were a common depository for cash, and one man hid a gold watch and ring in the stove. One frightened passenger went into the sleeping car and stretched out on the floor, dreading a confrontation with the robbers.

The engineer was forced to use the coal pick and break into the express car, where the express messenger, Archibald S. "Archie" Johnson, had armed himself with a pistol. Outside the door, Sizer heard the pistol being cocked and called out, "Don't shoot, Archie, it's me. He's making me do it!" The door was unlocked and opened. The bandit ordered Johnson to move some trunks out of the way, and he and the engineer entered the car. The messenger was ordered to put his pistol down, and he laid it on top of a box. Standing with the engineer in front of him as cover, the bandit ordered Johnson to open the express safe. The masked man threw Sizer a sack and ordered him to hold it open while Johnson deposited valuables from the safe into it. One of the items placed in the sack was a large book, and the bandit ordered it discarded, commenting that he was no bookkeeper. Johnson adroitly covered up with books and other documents over $1,700 that lay on the bottom of the safe. Once Johnson claimed the safe was empty, Sizer handed the sack to the bandit, and, as instructed, also handed over Johnson's pistol butt first. The bandit fired several shots down either side of the train to give the impression that there were several robbers instead of just one.

Conductor Elliott, armed with a pistol, called out to the passengers for any volunteers to go to the front of the train. Silence was his only response, so he set out alone for the express and baggage cars. He saw the flashes of gunshots being fired along the windows as he passed through the cars, and assumed that a band of robbers had control of the train. When he reached the express car, he was confronted by the bandit and his two pistols, with Johnson and Sizer between them. The robber called out, "You, big fellow, get back there or I'll kill you." Since a gunfight was impossible with the two trainmen between them, Elliott retreated back to the first class car.

Sizer was then ordered to return to the engine, told that he was free to pull out. The robber calmly turned away from the train and walked into the surrounding woods and darkness.[341] According to Agee, the bandit, Rube Burrow, made away with only $256.19.[342] The train chugged the short distance northeast a few miles to Brewton, arriving about eleven p.m., where Elliott telegraphed news of the robbery to his superiors. In turn, the Escambia County, Alabama, Sheriff was notified, as were Southern Express officials, including Agee. By the time the train pulled into Montgomery, a large crowd, including newsmen, were on hand to learn the details. A special engine, ridden by Agee and others, was sent down to the Escambia county sheriff, who had organized a posse with six bloodhounds to take up the pursuit of the robber.[343]

There was little doubt that Rube Burrow was the author of the Flomaton robbery. He had certainly been in Santa Rosa County just across the state line. For audacity, pulling a train robbery single-handedly was remarkable, it being similar to the same feat pulled by Eugene Bunch in November of 1888. Detectives converged at Flomaton where local posses had already spread out looking for Burrow. Nine men were stationed along the Escambia River in the hope that the river would not be an avenue of escape. The assumption was made that Burrow had ventured back to his sanctuary in the Florida swamps, and two search parties were organized to cross into Santa Rosa County. Agee, Tom Jackson, and another detective went to Milton, Florida, to set up a temporary headquarters, while another group of lawmen went on foot about twelve miles south of Flomaton where they found a small boat had been stolen, confirming the suspicion that Burrow had come that way.

The second posse, led by Detective Charles Kinsler, pressed on another thirty-five miles through canebrakes and swamps. On one of the few public roads in the area, they ran into a traveling minister who recalled seeing a man a day and half earlier at Black Water Creek who fit the fugitive's description. The posse returned to Milton to round up some horses, but Agee terminated the pursuit, likely with the realization that the wily Burrow had too much of a lead. Rumors began to spread that Burrow was teaming up with Eugene Bunch and other known outlaws. Reports of Burrow being seen in other localities resulted in detectives being hastily dispatched to those points to check them out. As in Texas, lawmen were stopping all suspicious men spotted in the countryside. Armed guards were placed on trains in the vicinity in anticipation that Burrow might try another robbery.[344] Various parties with bloodhounds scoured southern Alabama and the Florida Panhandle, but without success.[345] Southern Express Superintendent H.C. Fisher, exhausted from his efforts in the search, told the newspapers that he was satisfied that Burrow remained alone, not with Bunch or any others, and was safely back in Lamar County.[346]

On September 12, a party consisting of Tom Jackson, Kinsler, and two others, along with John Barnes as a guide, took a train from Flomaton to Good Range, south of Milton, Florida. The hope was to surprise Burrow at the Wells cabin. Moving at night over marshy wilderness under difficult conditions with little food, they arrived there after dark on September 15, moving up to within 400 yards of the cabin. Keeping well out of sight, the posse kept vigil for the next three days and nights, waiting for a sign of their quarry. They observed members of the Wells household periodically leaving the cabin, probably to make contact with Burrow, but the detectives decided not to follow them lest their presence be exposed. Finally, however, suffering from hunger and thirst, the detectives decided not to wait any longer. The Wells cabin was rushed at sunrise on September 18, but Burrow was not found inside.[347]

Barging into the cabin, the detectives confronted an outraged Wells. He adamantly denied that he had harbored Burrow in any way and refused to cooperate with them. The only other member of his family there, a daughter, reluctantly cooked breakfast for the famished posse after they indicated they would take food anyway. Wells' wife appeared at the cabin shortly after carrying a sack that had bread crumbs in it. The detectives suspected that she was returning from taking food to Burrow.

Despite the objections of the family, a search was made of the cabin. They discovered a trunk containing a suit of clothes, an overcoat, thirty-five dollars in stitched bills believed to have been taken from the Southern Express Company in the Flomaton robbery, and newspapers of various dates, many of which carried accounts of train robberies. They also found notes and letters addressed to "W.S. Ward," the name that Burrow had been using as an alias. Mrs. Wells attempted to claim the clothes as belonging to her sons, but finally admitted that they belonged to "Mr. Ward."[348] Wells claimed the cash and the detectives swapped other currency for it, also taking the clothes from the trunk with them.

The thought now was to try and deny Burrow any food or sanctuary. There was a sense that the hunt was drawing closer and Jackson and his men doggedly kept up the search. The Wells family remained under close scrutiny, and detectives checked various trails around the area for miles. After a few days, Jackson located a reliable source who told him that Burrow had left the Florida Panhandle swamps, crossing the Yellow River just across the Florida line on September 25. He called his detectives off the hunt, as well as Barnes, who had not been revealed to outsiders as being with the posse. Barnes returned to his home in Alabama, and the detectives returned to their respective headquarters.

Early on the morning of September 29, Burrow, still using the name Ward, showed up at Barnes' residence, unaware that Barnes lived there or of the role his former employer had just played. Barnes, however, did not know that and was sure that the fugitive was there to exact revenge. Burrow asked for something to eat, and a fearful Barnes invited him in and had him sit down at a table. Barnes went into the kitchen and told his wife that "That man is Rube Burrow, and I believe he has come here to kill me, and if he does so, you will know who murdered me." While his wife fixed some breakfast, Barnes, who had no firearms, excused himself and sent a message to a neighbor a half-mile away to come to his assistance, but the neighbor was not at home. Barnes went back inside.

The fact that Burrow showed up at the Barnes household was likely a bizarre coincidence. At the table, as Burrow ate breakfast, Barnes, knowing full well who his guest was, commented offhandedly that Burrow's face seemed familiar, suggesting that perhaps he had worked at a logging camp in Baldwin County in March of 1888. Burrow replied, "I guess not," and would not acknowledge that he knew Barnes, perhaps hoping, even if he did remember, that Barnes would believe he was mistaken. After finishing breakfast, Barnes provided Burrow with two days' provisions, for which the fugitive paid him liberally. Burrow asked for directions for various points, then left on foot. When the outlaw was out of sight, Barnes immediately went to Castleberry, in Conecuh County, where he telegraphed Southern Express officials: "Ward, the man you call Rube Burrow, took breakfast at my house this morning and left at noon, going by way of Repton, Ala. Send Jackson with sufficient force to capture him."[349]

Tom Jackson was immediately notified. Since Repton was northwest of Barnes' place, the detective calculated that Burrow was trying to make his way back to Lamar County. He received information that Burrow had inquired at several places along his northerly route as to spots where he might cross the Alabama River.[350] Accompanied by Detective Charles Kinsler and a detective from the Louisville & Nashville Railroad, also named Barnes, as well as some trained bloodhounds, Jackson headed for a likely crossing spot, Bell's Landing, which was situated on the Alabama River in the line of route to Lamar County from Castleberry.[351]

Several miles from Bell's Landing, in hilly country just a short distance southwest of present-day Hybart in Monroe County, John S. McDuffie[352] maintained a farm at nearby River Ridge. McDuffie, 37, had been suggested to Jackson by the Monroe County sheriff as a brave and reliable man. Looking for someone locally who knew the geography of the area, Jackson went to his farm. It was also reported that a boat belonging to McDuffie was believed to have been stolen by Burrow to cross the river, which was additional incentive for McDuffie to take part in the pursuit.[353] Since the detectives had maintained close surveillance over crossings on the Alabama River during the previous night, they were fairly sure that Burrow had not yet crossed. At about ten o'clock on the morning of Friday, October 3, while McDuffie was reconnoitering around Bell's Landing, an African-American messenger was sent from Mrs. McDuffie with word that Burrow was then eating breakfast at the cabin of another African-American two miles from the McDuffie's farmhouse, about six miles from the landing.

Putting whip and spur to his horse, McDuffie and those with him raced back to the farm and surrounded the cabin. They quickly discovered that Burrow had finished breakfast and taken a boat to cross the river. They were only about thirty minutes behind the outlaw. Burrow had slept in a bed of brush near the river the night before. While McDuffie and his men stood around the cabin figuring their next step, his wife and their six-year-old son walked up, having intended to get a good description of the outlaw to help the pursuers. A description was obtained from those at the scene, and it was revealed that Burrow was armed with three pistols and a rifle.[354]

In order to cross the Alabama River, Jackson and his men were forced to go six miles out of their way. They knew that they were not far behind the fugitive, and time was now critical. Their hope was that Burrow would forsake the swamps and take the one public road that led northward to Demopolis, which would take the fugitive through Marengo County. The lawmen hired a covered wagon and, joined by McDuffie, crowded together and ordered the driver to proceed. They remained hidden inside the wagon with the hope that they would overtake and surprise Burrow, leaping out bristling with firearms to capture the outlaw. The men traveled about ten miles until it grew dark. They stopped and camped, sending someone back to bring their horses up in order to resume the hunt the next day.[355]

On Saturday, October 4, the lawmen reached Thomasville, in Clarke County, and determined they were only about two hours behind Burrow. Telegrams were sent to express officials, who hastily made their way to Demopolis, believing they could intercept Burrow attempting to cross the Tombigbee River there on his way to Lamar County. Jackson figured that Burrow was staying off the public road, making his way on foot through the woods. The detective decided to go ahead with his men to Demopolis and organize guards there to see if they could intercept the fugitive coming north.

Early Sunday morning, October 5, Southern Express officers consulted with the detectives at Demopolis and it was decided to quietly organize additional posses to guard river landings, as well as make a search of portions of Marengo County south of Demopolis. They were convinced that Burrow had to be in that area, and Agee later wrote that "scores of the good people of that section joined in the chase."[356] By that evening, a swarm of searchers were looking through Marengo County for Burrow. At dawn Monday morning, it was believed that Burrow had yet to cross the Tombigbee. Knowing it was the outlaw's habit to seek food and shelter at the cabins of African-Americans, Jackson sent out word to area farmers to check on such sites on their property, as well as to enlist the assistance of their hired help.

At midnight Monday, Tom Jackson and John McDuffie rode back to Demopolis from their search, but there was no word that Burrow had been spotted. At three o'clock the next morning, Tuesday, October 7, a courier sent by D.J. Meadow reported to Jackson that Burrow had been spotted the evening before about three miles from Beckley's Landing on the Tombigbee River, just north of the small village of Myrtlewood. Jackson felt that Burrow might attempt a crossing of the river Tuesday night, and he and McDuffie rode the eighteen-mile distance to the landing, joined by volunteer Jefferson Davis "Dixie" Carter of Myrtlewood.

Carter, born in November of 1863, had been named for the former president of the Confederacy. Unmarried, he maintained a small fifteen-acre farm in Marengo County, as well as a small store in Myrtlewood. Described by Agee as "quiet and modest in his demeanor," he was unaware that he was embarking on a life-changing episode.[357]

Jackson rode along the west side of the river, searching for any sign that Burrow had crossed, and McDuffie did the same on the other side. By noon, all parties involved in the search had spread out, leaving McDuffie and Carter alone together.[358]

Jesse Hildreth, 45, in Agee's nineteenth century expression, was "a very worthy and reliable colored man." Alabama-born, he and his wife, Mariah, farmed in Marengo county near Myrtlewood.[359] Late Monday evening, October 6, he had seen smoke coming from the chimney of an abandoned "outhouse" near his own residence. Early the next morning, while looking for a horse, he went over and checked it out, finding Burrow asleep inside. Hildreth woke the sleeping man, asking him.

"Boss, what is you doing here?" Burrow told him that he was hunting work and asked him to get him some coffee. According to Agee, the black man felt that this was the fugitive that had the countryside turned upside-down and told the outlaw that he would go home and get some coffee for him.[360]

Hildreth located the loose horse then went home and got some coffee. He rejoined Burrow who appeared to be leaving, and in order to detain him until some assistance could come by offered to sell his horse to the fugitive. Burrow declined the offer and asked for directions to Blue Lick.[361] Determined to keep the fugitive in sight, Hildreth then offered to show him the way, inviting the bandit to ride his horse while he walked. At about noon a hard rain had commenced, and as the duo passed the cabin of another African-American, George Ford, Hildreth suggested that they stop, get out of the rain, and have lunch there. Ford lived in a small neighborhood known as Boneyville, about two miles east of Myrtlewood.[362]

While lunch was being prepared, Hildreth walked outside, hoping to see "some of the bosses," to assist in capturing the fugitive. Another African-American, Frank Marshall, who was part of the posses searching for Burrow, rode up to the cabin and Hildreth explained the situation. While the two were talking, they spotted McDuffie and Dixie Carter riding in their direction. The two black men joined them out of sight of the cabin and explained that Burrow was inside the cabin.

Since Ford's cabin sat in an open field, it was obvious that the two white men could not get within two hundred yards of the residence without being spotted by the cagey Burrow. A quick plan was hatched whereby Hildreth and Marshall would go into the cabin, seize Burrow, then McDuffie and Carter would come in on their signal.[363]

While the two white men took cover as close to the cabin as they could, Hildreth and Marshall returned. Burrow apparently thought nothing of another black man entering the scene. He was wrapping his Marlin rifle in an oil cloth, and Hildreth, thinking to get the weapon away from the bandit, offered to wrap it for him. Burrow handed over the rifle and Hildreth wrapped the weapon, making sure that the oil cloth was around the trigger in order to make it more difficult to fire. As Burrow reached for the rifle, Hildreth dropped it and threw his arms around the surprised bandit. Marshall leaped in to help subdue him. Hildreth was a large, strong-muscled man, but he had problems trying to hang on to the desperate Burrow. The outlaw buried his teeth into Marshall's shoulder as the trio struggled in the small cabin. Burrow could not get to a pistol across the room, but dragged his would-be captors across the floor, attempting to grab a fork off the table as a weapon.

Outside, McDuffie and Carter had crept close enough to hear the struggle, and rushed inside with guns drawn just as the three combatants finally crashed to the floor. Burrow was still frantically trying to free himself. McDuffie grasped the outlaw by the throat, choking him until he cried out, "I surrender! I surrender!" The captors found $178 in cash on Burrow, and recovered one pistol in addition to his Marlin rifle. The outlaw was quickly tied up with ropes and placed on McDuffie's horse, his hands tied in front and his arms tied against his body. His feet were bound together beneath the horse. Some accounts had Burrow trussed and laid across the horse, head on one side and feet on the other.[364] Bringing along Burrow's rifle, the four men then escorted Burrow the eight miles to Linden, the county seat of Marengo County, arriving there just at dark Tuesday evening.[365] For the first time in his criminal career, Rube Burrow was a prisoner of the law.

In 1934, writer Joel D. Jones recalled an 1890 interview he had with Jesse Hildreth in which Hildreth gave a slightly different account of the capture of Burrow. In that account, Hildreth said that he and Frank Marshall were at Ford's cabin when McDuffie and Carter rode by, telling them they were hunting a "tramp" who had stolen a boat, and were offering a $100 reward for him. Rube Burrow's name was not mentioned. According to Hildreth, "If we had known it was Mr. Rube, we would never [have] bothered him." Shortly after McDuffie and Carter left, Burrow was supposed to have been walking down the road toward the cabin. Assuming he was the "tramp" and figuring to nab him, they were going to tell Burrow that a rattlesnake had crawled under a log, invite him to kill it, then nab the man when he bent over to check the log. But, according to Hildreth, the man asked if they had anything to eat and he was invited inside the cabin.

Inside, Burrow set his rifle against the wall by the door and sat down at a table. Suddenly, Hildreth and Marshall grabbed him and a major struggle commenced. Burrow tried to reach his rifle, but it was kicked out the door. They finally were able to hold him down and tie him up with rope. Word was sent to McDuffie and Carter, who returned to the cabin. Burrow had offered the two black men fifty dollars if they would release him, but they declined, holding out for the $100 reward, and afraid of what the man might do once released. A greasy crocus bag that Burrow had been carrying was left by a stump outside when McDuffie and Carter took Burrow to Linden. When McDuffie addressed the tethered man as Rube Burrow, he denied it.[366]

On arrival at Linden, it was found that the Marengo County sheriff was out of town, and that he had the keys to the jail cells with him. McDuffie was not anxious to turn his prisoner over to the authorities just yet, at least not until the question of rewards was settled with the express company. Accordingly, the outlaw was taken to a room in the jail building, which was surrounded by a high brick wall. The prisoner's hands were still bound by ropes, and heavy iron shackles were placed around his ankles, a chain connecting them to a ring in the floor next to a bench on which Burrow sat.

McDuffie went to the town's telephone office and called express company officials at Demopolis, giving a full description of the prisoner. When he told the officials that they had recovered only one pistol from Burrow, they were concerned that he was mistaken, their last report being that he had three pistols when he crossed the Tombigbee River. McDuffie told them that Rube had said that he had sold the other two, but the officials were not convinced. "Rube never sells pistols." They also inquired about the sack Rube had been carrying and which had been left behind at Ford's cabin. McDuffie told them that it contained nothing but provisions. Thirty minutes after the prisoner was brought to Linden, George Ford found the greasy cloth sack, and knowing that it belonged to Burrow, brought it to Linden and left it on the courthouse steps. He told Hildreth about it, who relayed the information to McDuffie, but no one retrieved the sack. In Demopolis, Agee and fellow superintendent H.C. Fisher prepared to leave early Wednesday morning for Linden in order to confirm the capture of the wily outlaw.[367]

A crowd of townspeople, on hearing that the notorious Rube Burrow had been captured, flocked to the jail to see the bad man for themselves. Some food was brought to the jail for Burrow and his hands untied so that he could eat, but the leg shackles were left on. He joked with his captors as he ate, and visitors trooped through the jail to catch a glimpse of him. One of his visitors commented about his badly worn shoes, "Rube, your shoes are badly run down—you need a new pair." Rube responded, "Yes, some people always praise their shoes up, but I always run mine down." By midnight the excitement had died down and the crowd had disappeared. Carter was not feeling well, and taking Burrow's rifle and cash, went across the street to P.B. Glass' store to bed down for the night. Left behind were McDuffie with Hildreth and Marshall to guard their prisoner until the express officials and sheriff should arrive later on.[368]

It appeared that the reign of Rube Burrow, train robber and murderer, was finally at an end, much to the relief of train and express companies.

Chapter Seven

"I Will Paint Linden Red."

Marengo County Courthouse, Linden, Alabama. Author's Photo.

Rube Burrow in his coffin, Pinkerton Collection, Library of Congress (Courtesy of Richard Sheaff, Bethel, Vermont).

Rube Burrow in death. Pinkerton COllection, Library of Congress.

With the crowd gone, Rube Burrow, bound to an iron ring in the floor by the chains attached to his legs, was left alone with John McDuffie and his two black captors, Jesse Hildreth and Frank Marshall, one of whom went to sleep. Flickering coal oil lamps lit the scene in the Marengo County Jail at Linden as the trio waited for the dawn of Wednesday, October 8, 1890, and the arrival of the detectives. Burrow remained silent for some time, but gradually engaged his guards in conversation about the chase after him. McDuffie freely told him about the detectives swarming through the countryside, explaining that he likely would have been caught trying to cross the river if he had not been caught at Ford's cabin. Burrow expressed bitterness at detective Tom Jackson for his dogged pursuit, expressing delight that it was not Jackson that had caught him. He claimed he had over a hundred opportunities to kill Jackson, but had refrained from doing so. Now, he declared, he would kill Jackson and wanted him to know it.

The jail was a two-story brick building with a fifteen-foot outer brick wall surrounding it. There were three rooms on the lower floor. Burrow was held in the room to the right of the corridor, the Sheriff's office and the sleeping room of the deputy sheriff. The room had two doors, one opening into the corridor and the other into the jail yard. Burrow continued to be chatty with his captors. McDuffie asked him if he had held up the Flomaton train. "Maybe I did and maybe I didn't," responded the prisoner petulantly.[369] When someone read a newspaper description of him which stated that the bandit was balding, he invited them to feel his head: "I'll bet I've got the thickest hair of any man in town." His clothes were shabby and dirty, reflecting his experience hiding in the swamps and woods from the pursuing detectives. Burrow finally laid over on the bench as if to get some sleep, while McDuffie and one of the African-Americans remained on guard, the other black man going to sleep.

Sometime between three and four in the morning, Burrow told his captors that he was hungry. McDuffie told him that there was no way to get anything to eat at that hour; that dawn was not far off and at the normal time a good breakfast would be prepared for him. The bandit then asked about his crocus bag, saying that he had some candy and ginger snaps in it, and that he would share the snacks with them. Aware that the sack had been left by George Ford on the courthouse steps, McDuffie sent Jesse Hildreth after it. Hildreth later claimed that he brought the bag to Linden, not Ford, and left it outside the jail door. Without looking inside it, Hildreth placed the heavy bag between Burrow's feet.

Burrow dug in the sack, his hands being untied, and produced some candy, which he shared with the three men. McDuffie laid the pistol he had taken from Burrow down on a chair next to him. For about half an hour, the bandit ate candy along with them, then deftly dipped his hands once more into the greasy bag. Suddenly pulling out a heavy revolver, Burrow got the drop on his surprised captors, threatening to kill them if they made a move. Hildreth later said that at the sight of the pistol, "I seed myself lying in my coffin settin' on two poles at Pleasant Hill graveyard," and Marshall saw himself "talking to Saint Peter." The three men put their hands in the air. At Burrow's direction, Hildreth placed McDuffie's pistol on Burrow's lap and backed away. Covering the trembling three with both pistols, Burrow had Hildreth retrieve the key to his shackles from McDuffie's pocket and remove them from his legs.

McDuffie began to slowly move closer to Burrow, perhaps with a view to overpowering the bandit, even though Burrow was armed. But the outlaw detected the movement and told him, "That will do. Keep your distance or something might happen." McDuffie backed off saying, "Rube, the cake is yours."[370]

Burrow ordered McDuffie and Marshall to lie together flat on the floor, and Hildreth shackled their legs together and once more attached the chains to the iron ring in the floor. Hildreth was later quoted as saying that he also took handcuffs off Burrow and put them on McDuffie, although most accounts state that Burrow's hands were unrestrained.

The bandit, elated at his sudden freedom, took the key to the jailyard door from the chair where McDuffie had put it, and doing a little jig, crowed, "I have the big key to the jail. I am boss of the town, and as some people say I am not Rube Burrow, I will paint Linden red, and show them who I am." He told the two chained men that if they came out of the jail or raised any alarm, he would come back and kill them. Burrow then told Hildreth that he intended to find Dixie Carter and get back his rifle and his $178, though none of the men admitted they knew where Carter was staying. As the two left the jail, Hildreth adroitly dropped the keys to the shackles on the floor without Burrow seeing him do so. Burrow had Hildreth lock the door to the outside jail wall, and the key was left in the lock on the outside of the wall.

Once outside the jail, as dawn was faintly beginning to break in the east, Burrow ordered Hildreth to take him to Carter. With Hildreth carrying a lantern, Burrow directed him to take him to a local boarding house, but Hildreth pretended that he didn't know where it was located. Trying to stall for a while to allow McDuffie and Marshall time to free themselves and raise an alarm, the wily African-American stopped by every house along the route, waking the occupant, asking if Carter was there. They finally came to a boarding house owned by a man named McNeil. With Burrow hiding in the shadows, Hildreth managed to get someone to the door, who told him that Carter was not there. At the town's hotel, John Glass told the black man that Carter was not staying there either but was, instead, sleeping with the clerk at P.B. Glass' store. Almost an hour since the escape had now elapsed, and an anxious Burrow threatened to kill Hildreth "if I find you are fooling with me."

The two strode to Glass' store across the street from the jail and Rube knocked loudly on the door, then stepped aside out of view. He told Hildreth to tell whoever answered the door the express people had arrived and that McDuffie wanted him at the jail right away. A clerk named Dunn answered the door and told them that Carter was staying there. Awakened by the message that McDuffie wanted to see him at the jail, Carter, who was in the rear of the store, quickly dressed, putting his .32-caliber "lemon squeezer" pistol in a hip pocket. He walked out the front door, locking the store behind him. As Carter stepped from the door, Burrow appeared in front of him with pistol leveled, demanding his rifle and money, and threatening to "shoot his head off."

Carter realized immediately what was happening and said, "okay," then quickly reached for his pistol. The next few seconds are obscured by differing accounts. Both men fired at each other. Hildreth said that Carter got off the first shot, but Burrow fired almost simultaneously. Carter received a serious wound in the left shoulder, but, in spite of his injury, advanced on Burrow, who was backing up in the street, shot in the stomach. Burrow dropped one of his pistols and Hildreth picked it up and joined in the fray, getting off two shots that failed to hit anything. Burrow, backing away, got off five shots—one round merely snapped—then turned and staggered about ten paces. After a small leap in the air, he fell on the opposite side of the street at a large gate in the middle of the courthouse yard without saying a word, a small pool of blood seeping from beneath him. Hildreth said he heard him groan once or twice. Carter fell to his knees in the street, moaning in pain as W.W. Harden reached the scene, followed by C.B. Cleveland. Harden and two African-Americans moved Carter into Glass' store, while McDuffie, who had finally freed himself, Cleveland, and another African-American moved Burrow's body.[371] One later account claimed that Hildreth flung himself on Burrow's body as if to hold him down. When told to get up, Hildreth is supposed to have responded, "Naw sir, dis here man possumin'; he git up from heah an' kill everybody in dis town."[372]

McDuffie and Marshall had earlier managed to free themselves by breaking out the brick around the iron ring in the floor, then using the key to release the chain shackles. They left the jail and went looking for weapons, returning to the jail just in time to see the shooting across the street. Rube Burrow was dead. Only one of Carter's rounds had struck the bandit, entering the abdomen and severing an artery, causing almost instant death.[373]

Burrow's cavalier decision, once freed, to try to track down Carter and retrieve his rifle and money, rather than take what little time he had to put as much distance between himself and Linden was a fatal error in judgment. Word of his capture must certainly have caused a relaxation in the search for him, and he could have stolen a fleet horse and been miles away by the time the alarm was given. Perhaps the repeated escapes in the past had led him to believe in some sort of invulnerability to capture, that he was not destined to be caught because he was always able to outwit his pursuers. But the odds caught up with Rube Burrow and he finally ran in to someone with the nerve and courage to take him on. The Rube Burrow gangs were no more, and the leader was dead, two months and three days shy of his thirty-fifth birthday.

Newspapers across the country on Wednesday, October 8, unaware of the escape attempt, trumpeted Burrow's capture. An inquest was held over the body by Justice of the Peace John E. Hecker, and the jury, which included P.B. Glass, readily found that the outlaw had come to his death by a pistol shot fired in self defense by J.D. Carter. The body was then embalmed with alcohol and immediately turned over to Southern Express Superintendents Agee and Fisher, who, after securing a cheap pine coffin, placed it in a hack and carried it to Demopolis.[374] When John McDuffie expressed embarrassment at being outwitted by his captive, Agee observed that everyone makes mistakes, but "all's well that ends well."[375]

The officials arrived at Demopolis about five in the afternoon, at which time the coffin was opened and a curious crowd of some 500 people filed by to take a look at him. One account said that souvenir hunters took buttons from his shirt, hair from his head, and even his shoes were supposedly stolen.[376] As one witness melodramatically recalled the sight:

> In every feature was portrayed the character of the man, the whole making one of the most repulsive countenances to be met with in a life time. Mercilessness, shrewdness, brutality, and yet even in death how those grey eyes seemed to flout at fear.[377]

An exhausted but relieved George Agee told the press, "The others are all dead or in prison, and now I feel that I can take a little rest. I tell you we feel relieved to be safely rid of the last of them for they have given us no little trouble." At 8:45 a.m. Thursday morning, the body left by train from Demopolis through York, Alabama, to Birmingham.[378] Arriving at the Birmingham depot around 3:30 Friday morning, despite the early hour, local policemen were stationed around the express office to keep the large expectant crowd back. The coffin was taken from the baggage car on a wagon and quickly taken inside the express office. The hundreds of morbid spectators thronged against the office window, forcing a decision to open the coffin and let the crowd file by. An unidentified man gazed at the dead man in the coffin and, with tears in his eyes, said "It is Rube. I am sure now; poor Rube, he died game."

Once the crowd had thinned down to a few, the office was ordered cleared and the coffin was stood up in a corner so a photographer named Horgan could take some pictures. The body was posed with his rifle and pistols, and with his large black slouch hat. Someone remarked that Rube could almost be seen to move from his coffin.

At seven a.m., the body was put aboard a Kansas City, Memphis and Birmingham train for Sulligent, the nearest town in Lamar County to Vernon with a railroad, where it would be turned over to the family. Several hours after the train left, two men dashed into the express office inquiring if Burrow's body had been shipped. When told that it had already been shipped to Lamar County, the men hurriedly left, intending to get there and approach Burrow's father about purchasing the body for exhibition, "prepared to pay a good price for it." One of the pistols Burrow had been carrying, a .38-caliber Colt revolver taken from Messenger Archie Johnson during the Flomaton robbery and which was fired in the duel with Dixie Carter, was later returned to Johnson.[379] Agee subsequently provided copies of the Burrow death photographs to the *Chattanooga Evening Press* for display in its windows.[380]

A telegram was sent to Allen Burrow to expect his son's body at Sulligent at about noon, Friday. On arrival of the train, the old man was waiting, along with a crowd that blocked all of the streets around the train station.[381] He had received news of Rube's capture while on his way to market cotton at Sulligent, and took the news of his death philosophically.[382] A Southern Express official expressed a feeble apology: "We are sorry to bring your boy back in this shape, but it was the best we could do." Allen Burrow surmised, "I have no doubt that he was mobbed." On the same day, Reuben Houston Burrow was brought back to Vernon and buried in the Friendship Cemetery, four miles northeast of the town and not far from the family home, and the same place where he recruited Reuben Smith to join him in his robbery plans. Rube's weapons were taken to the Memphis office of the Southern Express Company where their exhibition was the object of widespread interest.[383]

And now the mythmaking began in earnest. Burrow's body was still warm when the *Montgomery Advertiser* declared:

> The name of Reuben Burrows [sic] belongs to history. He made a record and left it—a record that will go down to history as the most startling and romantic chapter in the criminal annals of this country. Single-handed and alone Rube Burrows dared and did more than any outlaw who ever figured in these United States.[384]

The *New York Sun* published a lengthy article on Sunday, October 12, detailing its version of the life of Rube Burrow, "a man of great determination and will power, combined with the reckless, daring nature of a ferocious beast." The article's accuracy can be questioned since it was written by E.W. Barrett of the *Atlanta Constitution* and included the alleged interview of Rube published in November of 1889. A year later, the *Constitution* observed, in discussing criminals such as Burrow, "The daring, the mystery, the romance of their deeds captivate a certain order of minds," and even in some cases encourage imitators.[385]

But controversy surrounding Burrow continued. On October 12, the *Birmingham Age-Herald* expressed remorse that "the manner in which his body was packed in a rude pine box, his clothing covered in mud, his long hair and beard matted and tangled is a sad commentary on his captors." According to an unstated source, Burrow's body was "flung off" the train at Sulligent "at the feet of his aged parents and kinsmen . . . an indication of heartlessness which bears a striking resemblance to the outlaw's own character." But it got worse. The article went on to claim that the outlaw had not been shot, there being no indication on his clothing or body that a bullet had entered him. Instead, it was claimed that his skull was broken and that his neck had been broken through strangulation, the implication being that he had been lynched.[386] However, the next day the *Age-Herald* printed a letter from its correspondent at Vernon that denied that Burrow's body was mutilated in any way, the allegations being fervently denied by express officials.[387] Nothing more was made of the claim.

Perhaps for the sake of personal notoriety, one attorney in Greenville, in south central Butler County, Alabama, notified the press that he had prepared Rube Burrow's will. According to him, Rube left an estate of $20,000, supposedly located in Alabama, Louisiana, and Mississippi, to his two children. A story was also broadcast by the *Mobile Register* that two days before the Flomaton robbery, Burrow approached another attorney named Green in Brewton, Alabama, identified himself, and asked the lawyer to prepare his last will and testament.[388] There is no record that Burrow was ever in Butler County, nor has either of these alleged wills surfaced. And notoriety circled over the heads of the Burrow family, perhaps including the two men who wished to buy Rube's body. In a notice in the *Vernon Courier*:

> The family of Reuben Burrow very justly complain of the many inquiries made of them about Rube, and are at all times made to gratify the curiosity of the questioner, and inquirers [*sic*] are made with such indifference to the feelings of the family, that it has become unpleasant to them to talk on the subject, and the *Courier*, at the request of the family, makes known the fact.[389]

A photographer visited Vernon several weeks after the burial to gather pictures for illustration of a book detailing the life and history of the bandit. The *Courier* observed that it would likely be stale reading as the only information the author had was from newspaper accounts.[390]

It was alleged by one Southern Express official, contrary to the family's desire for privacy, that the family had Rube's body disinterred so that his clothes could be removed and sold for twenty dollars, as well as a plaster cast taken of his face so that a traveling exhibition could be pulled together to tour the country.[391] A Vernon lawyer, F.S. Shield, affirmed that the family had sold to a dime museum the first coffin that Rube had been interred in, his body having been reburied,[392] but perhaps after removing his initial clothes. Allen Burrow confirmed that, on October 17, a suit of clothes belonging to Rube was "loaned" for exhibition at a state fair, to be returned at the close of the fair. However the clothing was taken to Montgomery for display at the Southern Exhibition, after which they disappeared.[393] There is no record that Burrow's body was disinterred, it being more likely that it was adorned with more appropriate clothing by the family prior to burial.[394]

However, it can safely be said that the citizens of Alabama were satisfied that the reign of the train robber in their state had come to an end. Governor Seay wrote to the Southern Express Company:

> The running at large of the outlaw was a menace not only to the State, but to this entire section of the country, and the ending of his career of crime is cause for congratulation to us all. Much as we would have preferred, by the regular course of law, to have marked a more ignominious end, his hardness,

his readiness and his desperation prevented this, but leaves to us the very satisfactory reflection that there was found in the lawful paths of life the courage, the presence of mind and the constancy which surpassed that of the outlaw himself.[395]

Moving quickly, the Southern Express Company, having spent thousands of dollars to fund the pursuit of Rube Burrow, as well as the losses realized through his robberies, now sought to recoup as much of those losses and expenses as it could. The company instructed its Savannah, Georgia, attorneys to institute a lawsuit against the Burrow family for any property that resulted from the robberies.[396] Although Lamar County deed records do not reflect it, it was said that Rube had invested $2,000 from the Duck Hill robbery in a farm on which his family was now living.[397] According to Agee, in his entire career of crime, Rube Burrow had garnered a total of only about $5,500 in loot. Of that, he was supposed to have spent about $400 to help his brother Jim buy land in Texas, then spent some $1,600 for the land that his father was now living on, the money paid supposedly coming from the Buckatunna robbery.[398]

The severely wounded Dixie Carter remained in Linden, unable to return to his home at Myrtlewood. Finally, during the first week of November, after spending ten days in Mobile for treatment, he returned home.[399] Unfortunately, Burrow's bullet through his left shoulder paralyzed that arm, a condition that would remain for the rest of his life. After a short period of recovery, he could only move this left thumb and forefinger, but the condition worsened. In December he returned to the Mobile hospital for another operation. By Christmas, though his arm remained paralyzed, he was physically able to go to Birmingham to meet with Southern Express officials about the pending rewards for Burrow's capture.[400] In April of 1891, while seeking treatment for his arm at the National Surgical Institute in Atlanta, Carter was asked if he would do it all again knowing he would lose his arm. "It is like gambling; I have had a taste of it and I feel pretty sure I would do it again."[401]

In the aftermath of the killing of Rube Burrow, the authorities geared up for the pending trials of Leonard Brock, alias "Joe Jackson," and Reuben Smith. On Tuesday, October 28, 1890, a deputy United States marshal was in Lamar County serving subpoenas on witnesses for both defendants' November 10 federal trials at Jackson, Mississippi, including Lamar County Judge of Probate W.A. Young and John Thomas Burrow.[402] As early as September, while the hunt for Rube Burrow was going on, John W. Wanamaker, the United States Postmaster General, concerned about the mistrial in Rube Smith's first federal trial, had urged United States Attorney General W.H.H. Miller to appoint Wayne County, Mississippi, District Attorney James H. Neville to assist United States Attorney Albert Lea in the prosecution. Neville was credited with successfully prosecuting Smith in the state trial, and his value stemmed from his acquaintance with the evidence and awareness of the defenses that might be thrown up. On September 3, Neville was appointed, he having agreed to accept a fee of $400 for his services.[403]

The prosecutors and Southern Express officials met on October 16 at the Jackson prison to discuss the upcoming trial of the two men. They all called on Leonard Brock in his cell, offering to have subpoenas issued for him should he change his mind and choose to plead not guilty. However, Brock asserted his intention to plead guilty, and, having no money, did not intend to hire a lawyer. Brock indicated a willingness to testify against Smith, but was bothered about how that would be perceived. "What will people think of me for doing that—see how the world looks upon Bob Ford?" Robert Ford had received instant notoriety and infamy for the assassination of Jesse James in April of 1882. The officials assured him that "all fair-minded and Christian people would applaud him for standing on the side of honesty and truth," but he concluded that Judas Iscariot was not given "a very fair name" in the Bible. Brock was often heard to say that "I prefer death to imprisonment for life, for what is life without liberty?"[404]

Two days before his Monday, November 10, trial, Brock offhandedly told a fellow inmate who had a worn-out old hat, "You need a new hat; you may have mine Monday." Around nine o'clock Monday morning, detective Tom Jackson and United States Marshal Mathews went to the penitentiary to bring Brock to the federal courthouse. Brock had been under special surveillance during his stay there, staying at night in a cell on the ground floor. However, during the day he had been permitted to occupy one of the guard rooms on the third floor of the prison, perhaps a perquisite granted to encourage his testimony against Smith. A prison guard was sent to bring him down from his cell to the prison sergeant's office.

As the guard was unlocking the door to the room, Brock signaled to a convict in the yard below and tossed a note out the window.

November 10th, 1890

> To all who may read this. I write this to inform you that my name is L.C. Brock; was born and raised in Coffee county, southeast Ala. And I am not guilty of the crime for which I am imprisoned. I am innocent, the God of Heaven knows it. I have suffered all the while for the crime of some one else. On the 29th of September I wrote to L.B. Moseley, Deputy U.S. Marshal, Jackson, Miss. to come and get the names of my witnesses. He has not come yet. I do not believe the letter was mailed to him at all. Through August I had fever and nothing to lay on up stairs (daytime) but the floor, fainted 25 or 35 times from weakness. I am telling this to show or give you an idea of how I have been treated. They intend to force me to a trial without my witnesses. You show this to any and all if you wish,
>
> Respectfully.
> L.C. BROCK[405]

When the guard unlocked the door and told Brock that he had come to escort him to the first floor office where Jackson and the marshal were waiting, Brock said "all right," and followed the officer out.

The penitentiary consisted of four tiers of cells, each with narrow galleries overlooking an eighty-foot-long rotunda or corridor, the fourth tier standing sixty feet above the corridor. As the guard and Brock reached the head of the stairs from the third tier, the prisoner suddenly pulled out a knife that he had made from an old file and hidden on his person and started to climb the stairs to the fourth tier, warning the guard to stay back or he would be cut. The sergeant of the prison was immediately notified and, accompanied by Mathews and Jackson, raced to the corridor beneath where Brock was walking back and forth along the fourth tier. They called out to Brock, asking what he was doing, and the prisoner calmly replied that he intended to jump and kill himself.

The note that Brock had thrown from the window was brought to the officials, who then asked Brock to whom he had given letters asking for witnesses to be summoned. Brock ignored the question and accused the Southern Express Company of "railroading" him into either the death penalty or life imprisonment, without allowing him to defend himself. Mathews told him that he could have a lawyer and that he, personally, would see that the witnesses he wanted would be summoned.

Brock still refused to come down and continued to threaten his intention to jump. He then moved an old sewing machine stand next to the balcony railing and stood on it, declaring that he was "alone and friendless," and preferred death to life in prison. The officials were struck with how cool and deliberate the man was, he not displaying any degree of distress in his demeanor. He asked that Harrell, his uncle who was still in Jackson, be telegraphed as to Brock's death and that his body be sent to his mother.

The confrontation now having gone on almost an hour, Sergeant Montgomery, the prison supervisor, deciding to make a move, took off his coat and hat and began climbing the latticed walls while the others diverted Brock's attention. His intention was to reach the fourth floor, upset the table on which Brock was standing, and grab the prisoner before he could regain his feet. But when he had reached the third tier, he was convinced that the effort was foolhardy and he would likely be stabbed by Brock before he could accomplish his mission. He returned to the ground corridor. Brock admitted that he had received fair treatment by prison officials.

In another ploy, the officers questioned Brock's manhood in taking a cowardly way out, but it did no good. At one point, Brock declared his desire to make a statement if a reporter was present, and Rube Smith, who could hear what was going on from his cell, called out to the prison sergeant to let him make the statement.

However, Jackson and Marshal Mathews had slipped silently to the stairway and quickly reached the fourth tier, standing some six feet from Brock, pleading with him to drop the knife and come downstairs with them. Jackson edged forward several more feet, asking, "Joe, you are not going to jump, are you?" "Yes, I am!" he replied, and, throwing his derby hat before him, suddenly sprang head first over the railing. He spun over in the air as he fell the sixty feet, the back of his head and shoulders striking the brick floor below with a sickening splat. He missed by a few inches a mattress that officials had brought out in the desperate hope that they could minimize injury. Though unconscious, he only lived another hour. At about five that afternoon, he was buried in the prison cemetery. In his pocket, officials found the following poem:

> How wise we are when the chance is gone,
> And a glance we backward cast.
> We know just the thing we should have done
> When the time for doing is past.[406]

It was said that when told about Rube Burrow's death, Brock had broken down and cried. The fact that he had confessed against his cohorts had weighed heavily on his mind. Under the impression that he and Burrow had been betrayed by others, he had weakened, he later said, and gave his detailed confession. When he found out from talking with Rube Smith in prison that no one in the Burrow family had admitted anything, that the detectives had lied to him, he felt duped and saw his treatment as unfair. As a result, he saw as his only choice to life imprisonment was to commit suicide rather than carry out his agreement to testify against Smith. His confession could not be used as evidence against Smith after Brock's death, so his code of honor seemed to dictate to the distraught man that death was his only option.[407]

Only two hours after Brock's violent death, Reuben Smith went on trial before federal Judge R.A. Hill for robbing the mail in the Buckatunna robbery. Prosecutors Lea and Neville presented as witnesses the Buckatunna train men, as well as Neil McAllister, who had allowed the robber to stay in his cabin. The letters written by Smith that he attempted to smuggle to his father were also introduced into evidence. For the defense, Rube Smith's father and uncle, James Smith and James Barker, testified that Rube was with them when the robbery occurred.[408] The trial took five days, and on Friday, November 15, the jury received the court's charge at ten in the morning and took only half an hour to return a verdict of guilty.[409] In addition, Smith's father and uncle were promptly charged and arrested for perjury. They immediately pleaded guilty and James Smith was sentenced to one year and Barker to two years confinement in the Detroit House of Corrections.[410]

On Tuesday, November 18, the federal judge sentenced Smith to life imprisonment. Imploring Smith to obey "strictly all the laws of God and man, and especially the regulations of the prison," Judge Hill held out the possibility that he might someday receive a presidential pardon.[411] His sentence was to be served at the state penitentiary at Columbus, Ohio. It was felt that the House of Corrections in Detroit, Michigan, where federal prisoners were usually sent, was not sufficiently secure to hold a desperate criminal like Smith, who had a record of escape attempts.[412] The governor of Mississippi, eager to rid his penitentiary of a desperate train robber, was only too glad to turn him over to the prison in Ohio.[413]

With a heavy escort of federal marshals, Rube Smith was taken from Jackson en route for Columbus, Ohio, on Monday, December 8. Accompanying them, headed for prison in Detroit, were his father and uncle.[414] On December 10, Smith was received at the Columbus prison and assigned number 21849.[415] The last member of Rube Burrow's criminal saga was now behind bars.

Chapter Eight

"Nip Was a Corker"

Rube Burrow's erroneously spelled grave marker, Fellowship Cemetery, Lamar County, Alabama. Author's Photo.

With the death of Rube Burrow and the imprisonment of Rube Smith, the question of rewards became an immediate concern. The Post Office had a standing offer of $1,000 for the arrest and conviction of anyone who robbed the mails. The dilemma was that Burrow was killed, not convicted. Jesse Hildreth and Frank Marshall, the actual captors of Burrow, received $100 each from John McDuffie as he had promised.[416] Of the $2,500 in rewards jointly offered by the express and railroad companies, $1,000 partial payment was initially made to Dixie Carter on December 20, 1890, in Birmingham.[417] How the remainder would be distributed was yet to be determined.

John McDuffie had been initially advised by John Anderson of Linden, Carter's lawyer, that the entire reward would amount to only about $900. Given such a low sum, as well as the severity of the injury to Carter, McDufffie waived any interest in claiming a part of that amount. However, the Southern Express Company subsequently called a conference of all interested parties, and McDuffie, now aware that a more significant amount of money was on the table, announced his intention to claim one-third of the amount. One account stated that there was a total of $7,500 offered by the Southern Express Company, the Mobile and Ohio and Illinois Central Railroads, the St. Louis, Arkansas and Texas Railroad, the U.S. Post Office, and the states of Arkansas and Mississippi.[418] To avoid any liability, the companies decided to let the parties work out the proportion of the split between themselves before paying them anything.[419] McDuffie subsequently waived any claim to rewards after receiving $500 from the Mobile and Ohio Railroad.[420]

Burrow had been dead but two months, but by Christmas of 1890 Southern Express Superintendent George Agee, who was a significant player in the hunt for the bandit, was already marketing a prospectus for his book. Titled *Rube Burrow, King of Outlaws, and His Band of Train Robbers*, the 194-page book, due out at the first of 1891, was to be published by The Henneberry Company in Chicago. According to the prospectus, the book "has not been attempted to weave a halo of romance about the deeds of Rube Burrow, but rather to give a narrative of facts in which the truth is found to be stranger than fiction."[421] Agee was later quoted as saying he wrote the book primarily to refute a Birmingham news account that Rube Burrow had netted $4,000,000 from the Southern Express Company in his robberies. He calculated that Rube would have garnered the same amount as actually taken if he had worked at "honest toil" for seventy-five dollars per month during the same time period.[422]

In August of 1891, the Post office finally came to a decision as to its payment of $3,000 in rewards to the parties. Dixie Carter would receive $1,000 for the capture of Burrow, and Tom Jackson, the detective, $1,000 for the capture of Rube Smith. The remaining $1,000 would be split six ways for the capture of Leonard Brock to Tom Jackson, Lee Metcalfe, S.F. Pennington, John Jackson and J.M. Parchman of Aberdeen, Mississippi (associates of Tom Jackson), and Jack Gathings of Gate City, Alabama.[423]

The Post Office finally resolved its dilemma in awarding an amount to Dixie Carter, concluding that Burrow's conviction would more likely have occurred had he been taken alive. Carter's $1,000 was designated as a "special award" in recognition of his bravery and life-altering injury, but not a "reward, in conformity with any general offer promulgated by this Department." In notifying Carter of this grant, E.G. Rathbone, an Assistant Postmaster General, while stingily keeping a limit on rewards paid out by the Post Office, commiserated on what he perceived as neglect in granting additional reward money to Jesse Hildreth, suggesting that perhaps Carter might consider sharing some of his money:

> I will thank you to convey to the two colored men, who rendered assistance in the capture, the appreciation which this Department feels at the part they took therein, especially to Jesse Hildreth, one of them, who so bravely stood his ground when the fusillade was in progress between you and Burrows, and joined in the attack, which resulted in his death.
>
> Although the receipts of the said two colored men are on file with your papers, as evidence that they were paid $100 each for the services rendered by them, and waived all claims to any share in the $1,000 which is now being paid to you, yet it strikes me that, in the case of Jesse Hildreth, he is deserving of additional money recognition at your hands, for his act in giving you support at the risk of his life was entirely voluntary on his part, and formed no part of the service performed by

him and his companion at the time Burrows was captured in the log cabin, and for which he was paid the one hundred dollars referred to.[424]

Bill Brock, now a free man, turned up in Dallas in November of 1891. Calling himself a detective, he visited the office of Dallas Police Chief James C. Arnold. Brock reveled in recounting his involvement in train robberies with Rube and Jim Burrow, describing Rube as "the big man of it all and was as good game as any man who ever lived." He described train robbery as an easy task. "It was all just as easy as falling off a log backward, once you know how, and have got the nerve to back up your knowledge of the fine art." Commenting on the fact that Nep Thornton had never been apprehended after he jumped bond in June of 1888, he observed:

> Nip [sic], he said, was a corker, and occasionally when things got hot would retire to his farm in Stephens county, Texas, and converting it into a fortress, defy anything short of a regiment of infantry to come and take him. The place was on the open prairie, where a man could be seen for miles and miles in daylight. Thornton ranged from the Indian Territory to the gulf, and from Louisiana to Arizona. He has many friends who have shared the spoils of his avocation, and will stand by him until his last day in the a.m.[425]

At about this same time, it was speculated that Thornton was still in the business of robbing trains, allegedly helping the Dalton brothers in the Indian Territory. However, after he jumped bond, Nep Thornton disappeared from sight and was permenently lost to history.[426]

A news story was spread around the country about this same time that caused an old rumor to resurface. It was claimed that the grave in which Jim Burrow had been allegedly buried at the Little Rock prison in October of 1888 was found to be empty when prisoners' bodies were being disinterred for removal to a new site. The implication was that he had escaped from the penitentiary. It was even reported that Jim's skeleton was hanging in the office of a young doctor in Little Rock.[427] The Arkansas authorities continued to insist that Jim Burrow had indeed died in 1888 and that the "empty grave" was not the one in which he had been buried.

Allen Burrow petitioned the Lamar County Probate Court in October of 1891, a year after Rube's death, asking for letters of administration so that Rube's small estate, initially estimated at a value of about a thousand dollars, could be settled with respect to his two children. Rube had left no will, contrary to the claims of several lawyers at the time of his death. Adeline Burrow, Rube's widow, was deemed to have declined to administer the estate by virtue of the lapse of time that had occurred, and apparently the family had not been in contact with her in Texas. An appraisal of his estate listed an estimated sixty dollars worth of personal property, including two cows, and $900 in real estate, all of which were awarded to Rube's two children.[428]

In other court action, in March of 1895, Allen Burrow also obtained a judgment in the Lamar County circuit court against the Southern Express Company for $294. The lawsuit had been brought to compensate the family for the cost of Rube's firearms, the team of oxen sold in Florida, and money taken from Rube's person at Linden. It was a short-lived victory, however, as two days later the company was awarded a judgment against Allen Burrow in the amount of $5,033.97 to compensate it for the plunder that Rube had taken in his robberies and allegedly transferred to the family.[429] It was a simple matter of examining Lamar County deed records to discover that, shortly after the Duck Hill robbery in December 1888, Rube had sent his parents at least $1,600, which they used to purchase land.[430]

In probating Rube Burrow's small estate, Allen Burrow had claims against it including not only the judgment of the Southern Express Company, but also such expenses as taxes paid on the property, digging a well, and repairs. In May of 1895 the estate was declared insolvent to handle the claims against it, and in July Allen Burrow was replaced as administrator. The various real property parcels in Rube's estate were sold off in December, the proceeds amounting to a total of $149.75. The Southern Express Company, desirous of gaining some payment on its judgment, closely monitored probate proceedings through the years, protesting when it thought an improper claim was being made. In January of 1897, when the estate was finally settled, the Southern Express Company was awarded $87.22, the money remaining in the hands of the administrator after all other approved claims against the estate were paid off. There is no record that the company ever received any further payments against its judgment.

Reuben Smith had not been long at the Columbus, Ohio, penitentiary before he began complaining of kidney trouble.[431] He apparently suffered on and off for four and a half years, when, on Saturday, April 20, 1895, he died in the prison hospital at the age of 30. He was diagnosed as having expired from Bright's Disease, a general description given in the 19th century to a variety of kidney diseases that took the form of severe back pain, high blood pressure, and vomiting and fever, as well as death.[432] Smith was buried at Green Lawn Cemetery in Columbus, Ohio, on April 22, his name mistakenly shown on the cemetery register for over one hundred years as "Rohben Smith."[433]

By the turn of the century, even the pulp novels ceased featuring Rube Burrow as a protagonist, while other outlaws lived on in romantic memory. Unlike Jesse James, Billy the Kid, and Butch Cassidy, Burrow had no champions who continued to trumpet his exploits and derring-do that kept him alive in the public mind. The era of the train robber passed soon thereafter, and Burrow was relegated to only occasional mention, two books about him last being published in 1981. Individuals who had been a part of the Rube Burrow story, including family, resumed normal lives, deliberately not reflecting on those years spent when he was the center of their circle. Fanciful stories about Burrrow began to crop up, as they did concerning any prominent outlaw after their deaths. In those areas that remembered him through the years, such as Lamar County, fact and fiction became confused. But outside Lamar County, Rube Burrow, who once was responsible for national headlines and comment as "King of the Outlaws," became largely forgotten, his story muddled by error and myth. It is only for this reason, not the violence or even glamour of his crimes, if such there was, that the historical record deserves to be set straight.

Afterword

Rube Burrow left behind many people closely involved with him and his crimes. The following is a short follow-up on those individuals.

George Washington Agee. Agee was born on September 14, 1846, in Buckingham, Virginia, to Benjamin Hooper Agee and Ann Elizabeth Mitchell. His first wife apparently died, and he married Kate Wheatley Saunders in December 1893. He was a superintendent for many years for the Southern Express Company. "His cool, quick mind and imposing carriage, and the unmistakable stamp of the Virginia gentleman, wins him prestige in every circle. The Agees were among the early Huguenot settlers on [the] James River." In 1900 he was living with a son-in-law, Dudley Saunders, in Memphis, Tennessee. He died on March 14, 1909.[434]

Henderson B. Alverson. Rube Burrow's first father-in-law was born July 10, 1816, in Surry County, North Carolina, to Elijah and Nancy Cook Alverson. Orphaned, he left home at an early age and apprenticed to a hat maker in Alabama. On January 3, 1836, he married Sarah Minerva Thompson, the mother of Virginia (Rube's wife) and Nancy (Nep Thornton's wife). He and his family lived in Alabama and Mississippi, settling in Shackelford County, Texas, about 1858. He served in 1861 as a Confederate soldier in the Mississippi infantry, but was discharged because of illness and because his family was "defenseless" on the Texas frontier. He moved his family to Tarrant County where he operated a water-powered grist mill on the West Fork of the Trinity River as well as ran a farm. Sarah Alverson died on June 23, 1869, and he married Louisa Holt on January 29, 1870, a marriage which ended in divorce in July 1879. On December 25, 1880, the 64-year-old Alverson married Drucilla Roberts, 19. He died on November 22, 1910, while living with his son James, and is buried in the Dido Cemetery in northwest Tarrant County.[435]

James Harrison Askey. He was born April 14, 1842, to farmer John and Casander Askey. In 1850 and 1860 the family was living in Hunt County, Texas. On July 6, 1861, he enlisted in the 22nd Texas Confederate Cavalry. After the war, on June 24, 1866, he married Sarah T. Williams in Hunt County. By 1880, he and his wife and their three children, plus some in-laws, were living in Callahan County, Texas, where he farmed. By 1900 the family had moved to Stonewall County, Texas. In 1910 he and his wife were living with one of their children at Jayton, in Kent County, Texas. In 1920 he and his wife were living at Kress Village, Swisher County, Texas, where he died of influenza on February 23, 1926.[436]

Cornelius H. "Neil" Bray. This compositor for the *Montgomery Advertiser* was born about 1859 in Virginia to Patrick and Lucy Chappell Bray, his father being from England. He subsequently was a printer in Birmingham, Alabama. He married his wife, Lillie, about 1884, and they had at least seven children. He survived his serious wound and died in Birmingham in June 1933.[437]

Elizabeth Victoria Acker Brock. Wife of William L. Brock, she was born on November 8, 1867, to Joseph Benn Acker and Martha Belzora Jones Acker in Cherokee County, Texas. She married Bill Brock in Erath County on March 27, 1885, and they had seven children. She died on February 17, 1949, in Potter County, Texas.[438]

William Lawrence Brock. He was born in Franklin County, Georgia, in April of 1856 to farmer James M. and Jane Brock, one of four children. By 1870 the family was living in Brazos County, Texas. On May 27, 1885, Brock married Elizabeth V. Acker in Erath County, Texas. After his run-ins with the law, he and his wife and four children were living in Dallas County, Texas, in 1900, where he worked as a carpenter. In 1910 the family consisted of five children (and living next door to a sixth) living at Plainview in Hale County, Texas. In 1920, still working as a carpenter, Brock and his wife and one child were living at Amarillo in Potter County, Texas. He died there on April 2, 1926.[439]

Marion Henderson Brumley. This cohort of Rube Burrow was born in McNairy County, Tennessee, on December 2, 1844, to farmer James C. and Melinda Majors Brumley, one of seven children. In 1844 the family came by covered wagon to Texas, settling first in Titus County, then moving to Erath County. During the Civil War, he served as a private in Company H of McCord's Frontier Regiment of the Texas Cavalry, mustering in at Breckenridge on July 17, 1863. Three days later he married Louisa Jane "Lou" Keith, born June 23, 1850, in Hunt County. After the war he returned to Erath County, and by1870 he and his wife had three children, ages 4, 1, and five months. In 1872 through April 10, 1874, he served with his brothers Calvin and William as minute men in a company organized to scout for Indians, commanded by a man named O'Neal. By 1880 his occupation was that of a cattle drover, and at home in Erath County he and his wife had eight children. Brumley's wife died on October 5, 1914. On July 18, 1915, he married Mrs. E.J. Tidwell in Alexander, Texas, and they made their home in Hermleigh, Scurry County, Texas. As of 1938, he was living with a daughter in Brown County. He died in Abilene, Taylor County, Texas, on November 28, 1940.[440]

Adeline A. Hoover Burrow. Rube's second wife was born in September 1859 to James Abraham and Nancy Elvira Underwood Hoover, the seventh of ten children. James Hoover reportedly served in the Civil War and was later blinded and burned during a house fire. In 1860 the family was enumerated in Gilmer, Upshur County, Texas, and in the Osage Township, Benton County, Arkansas, in 1870. In 1880 they were in Alvarado, Johnson County, Texas. She married Rube Burrow in Erath County on December 30, 1886, but they had no children and indications are that they separated fairly soon and she returned to her parents' home. In the 1900 census she was living with her aged parents in the Chickasaw Territory (now Oklahoma), still with the Burrow surname. In 1901 she married John W. Booker, eleven years her junior, and reportedly had one son, Jim Tilman Booker. They were living in Pottawatomie County, Oklahoma, in 1910 and 1920, although no child is listed with them in the census for those years. In 1916 and 1919, the two were living in Shawnee, Oklahoma. She died on November 26, 1932, three days shy of her 72nd birthday, and is buried at Waurika, Jefferson County, Oklahoma.[441]

Allen Henry Burrow. The father of Rube Burrow was born on May 21, 1825 and died on June 19, 1899, in Vernon, Alabama. He married Martha Caroline Terry in August 1849, and the family subsequently had five boys and five girls, including Reuben and James. Allen is buried next to Rube in the Fellowship Cemetery in Lamar County, Alabama.[442]

Joel Burrow. Rube Burrow's uncle was born on September 2, 1819. He was a farmer in what became Lamar County, Alabama. During the Civil War, like his brother Allen, he served in the Confederate Army. Sometime around 1873, he and his wife, Martha, moved their family to Wise County, Texas, where he purchased acreage for his farm on the West Fork of the Trinity River. By 1880 he and his wife had at least five children with them. Joel Burrow died on December 9, 1892, and is buried in the Fellowship Cemetery in Lamar County, Alabama, near his brother and nephew.[443]

John Thomas Burrow. The brother of Rube Burrow, he was born on May 26, 1849. He married Martha Ann Cash on August 25, 1872, and by 1880 they had five children. During the 1870s he and his family faced hard times on their farm. In 1877 he was indebted to D.A. Summers in Lamar County, Alabama, for $225, and subsequently was forced to turn over an ox wagon and yoke of oxen, ten hogs, and all household and kitchen furniture, including bedding and quilts, all to be sold at public auction. On May 28, 1889, he was the recipient of $1,600 from Rube to sell his brother some land. Martha Burrow died in 1892, and he remarried at least once. He died on June 3, 1933, in Tula, Lafayette County, Mississippi.[444]

Martha Caroline Terry Burrow. The mother of Rube and Jim Burrow was born in Alabama on January 17, 1828. After her husband, Allen, died in 1899, she lived with son William and his family in Lamar County. She next lived with her son-in-law James F. Hankins, who had married Martha Keziah Burrow. She died in Vernon, Alabama, on November 24, 1912.[445]

William Thomas Burrow. The son of Reuben Burrow, William was born in Texas on March 6, 1877. It is unknown when he left the household of Allen Burrow, having only five years of education, but by 1900 he was a laborer on the farm of Walter Derby in Tallahatchie County, Mississippi. He married within a few years after that, and by 1920 he and his wife, Ada, had five children and were living in Rosepine, Vernon Parish, Louisiana, where he was an oil field laborer. In 1930 he was still an oil field laborer, but the family was living in Jefferson County, Texas. By 1940, he and his wife were back in Rosepine. Burrow died there on November 17, 1945, at the age of 68.[446]

William Lewis Cabell. Cabell was born on January 1, 1827, in Danville, Virginia. He graduated from West Point in 1850 and served in the United States Army, reaching the rank of captain by 1858. On July 22, 1856, he married Harriet A. Rector at Fort Smith, Arkansas, and they subsequently had seven children. At the outbreak of the Civil War, he resigned his commission and enlisted in the Confederate Army with the rank of major. Later, as a brigadier general, called "Old Tige" by his soldiers, he was wounded in 1862, then became a prisoner of war in 1864. At the end of the war he became a lawyer at Fort Smith, then moved his family to Dallas, Texas, in 1872 where he worked as an insurance agent. In 1874 he was elected Dallas mayor and served as such until 1878. He served as United States Marshal for the Northern District of Texas from 1885 to 1889, then served as a general manager for a railroad. He died in Dallas on February 22, 1911.[447]

Jefferson Davis "Dixie" Carter. Carter was born in November of 1863 in Butler County, Alabama, to William and Susan Carter. As a young man he maintained a small general store at Myrtlewood in Marengo County, Alabama. In 1884 he paid 40 dollars for five acres in Marengo County, and in 1888 paid fifty dollars for ten more. He likely received no more than a total of $4,250 in reward money for the capture and death of Burrow. As a result of his wound, his left arm remained paralyzed for the rest of his life. On May 24, 1894, he married Lenora "Nora" McDuffie in Marengo County. They subsequently had five children. Dixie Carter died in a hospital in Selma, Alabama, on December 14, 1920, "as an indirect result" of the bullet fired by Rube Burrow in 1890.[448]

James Alexander Cash. Jim Cash was born about 1852 to Henry and Eliza Jane Cash. On November 13, 1870, he married Rube Burrow's sister, Sarah. He lived all of his life farming in Lamar County, Alabama, and sired at least four children. He died on February 20, 1910, in Lamar County.[449]

Jesse Hildreth. One of the captors of Rube Burrow in October 1890, Hildreth was born about 1835. He and his wife, Mariah, had five children as of 1880, living in Marengo County, Alabama. On April 27, 1892, he was shot and killed by Jack Singleton, another black man, when one of Singleton's "women" sought refuge at the Hildreth cabin when Singleton's cabin was flooded.[450]

Thomas V. Jackson. Tom Jackson was born about 1854 in Mississippi to Prince and Elizabeth Jackson. Just under six feet tall, he sported a neat brown moustache and enjoyed cigars. He served a number of years as a detective for the Southern Express Company. On August 21, 1892, he led a team of detectives in locating and shooting to death train robber Eugene Bunch in northeast Louisiana. He apparently married a second wife, Julia, around 1907. He died on February 15, 1924, at Memphis, Tennesee.[451]

Frank Marshall. One of the captors of Rube Burrow, the 1880 Marengo County, Alabama, census lists two Frank Marshalls, both married with children. One, 30, lived at Spring Hill; the other, 28, lived at Hills. Neither community exists today. It has been stated that Marshall died at Myrtlewood shortly after Jesse Hildreth, but no details are known.[452]

James McClung. Very little is known about James McClung. He was born about 1867 in Mississippi to Littleton Meaks McClung and his wife, Elizabeth. What happened to him after his testimony against Rube Smith is unknown.[453]

John McDuffie. One of the captors of Rube Burrow, he was born in August of 1852 in Alabama, the son of Archibald and Nancy Johnson McDuffie. About 1881 he married Virginia Marion Lett, who was born on October 27, 1857, at Burnt Corn, Alabama, to John Edward and Elizabeth Boykin Hunter Lett. The 1900 census lists seven children, one of whom later became an Alabama state representative. John McDuffie died sometime after 1900 and before 1910. Virginia McDuffie died on June 12, 1938, and is buried in the Johnson/McDuffie Cemetery at Monroeville, Alabama.[454]

Nancy Adeline Alverson Thornton. The wife of Napoleon Bonapart "Nep" Thornton, she was born to Henderson B. and Sarah Minerva Alverson in Double Springs, Okitebeha County, Mississippi on November 7, 1850. She was married to Thornton in Tarrant County, Texas, on August 29, 1869, and they had four children. Her sister, Virginia, married Rube Burrow. In an interview with her in Friona, Parmer County, Texas, in 1949, when she was ninety-nine years old, she recalled that in 1879, her husband rode off to look after his crops and she never saw him again. Actually, she and Nep were listed in the 1880 census for Erath County with two children, and he sold some property there in 1882. They also had a child born in 1884. She died at the age of 107 on December 11, 1957, and is buried in the West Park Cemetery at Hereford, Deaf Smith County, Texas.[455]

Napoleon Bonapart "Nep" Thornton. He was born on January 8, 1847, in Bienville, Louisiana, to Isaac and Tabitha Thornton, one of nine children. By 1860 he was in Erath County, Texas, living with his older brother David. He married Nancy Adeline Alverson, the sister of Virginia Alverson (who would marry Rube Burrow), on August 29, 1869. Initially living in Tarrant County, they subsequently had four children. On December 2, 1874, he bought 127 acres in Erath County for $350. In 1882 he sold some property, and in 1883 he and his wife sold the 127 acres for $700, less six acres that was sold as right-of-way for the Texas Central Railroad. He reported as estrayed in Erath County a red roan horse in 1883. Their fourth child, William Curtis Thornton, was born on January 14, 1884. At some point after this, according to his wife in 1949, he abandoned her and the family in 1879, but it is most likely that he disappeared when he jumped bond and fled. There is no record that he was ever retaken into custody. In 1900 the federal court ruled that the government was entitled to recover $3,000 and costs in a dispute over his forfeited bond. Without any documentation, his death has been listed as occurring in 1892.[456]

Bibliography

BOOKS

Acee, Joe. *Rube Burrows: Alabama's Most Famous Train Robber.* Vernon, Alabama: The Vernon Democrat, 1989.

Agee, George W. *Rube Burrow, King of Outlaws.* Chicago: The Henneberry Co., 1890.

Brant, Marley. *Jesse James: The Man and the Myth.* New York: Berkley Books, 1998.

Breihan, Carl W. *Rube Burrow: King of the Train Robbers.* West Allis, Wisconsin: Leather Stocking Books, 1981.

Carmer, Carl. *The Fine Art of Robbery.* New York: Grossett & Dunlap, 1966.

Carruth, Barbara Woolbright. *Rube Burrow: Alabama Desperado.* Sulligent, Alabama: Ms. B's Research Service, 2007.

Cushing, Marshall. *The Story of Our Post Office: The Greatest Government Department in All Its Phases.* Boston: A.M. Thayer & Co., 1893.

Harlow, Alvin M. *Old Waybills: The Romance of the Express Companies.* New York: D. Appleton-Century Co., 1934.

Harvey, Paul Jr. *Old Tige: General William L. Cabell, C.S.A.* Hillsboro, Texas: Hill Junior College, 1970.

Hoole, William Stanley. *The Saga of Rube Burrow.* University, Alabama: Confederate Publishing Co., 1981.

Horan, James D. *The Pinkertons: The Detective Dynasty That Made History.* New York: Crown Publishers, Inc., 1967.

Magee, Zuma F. *The Eugene F. Bunch Story.* Franklinton, Louisiana: Zuma F. Magee, 1975.

Miller, Rick. *The Train Robbing Bunch.* College Station, Texas: Creative Publishing Co., 1983.

_____. *Sam Bass & Gang.* Austin, Texas: State House Press, 1999.

Paddock, Capt. B.B. *A Twentieth Century History and Biographical Record of North and West Texas.* Chicago: The Lewis Publishing Co., 1906.

Patterson, Richard. *Train Robbery: The Birth, Flowering, and Decline of a Notorious Western Enterprise.* Boulder, Colorado: Johnson Publishing Co., 1981.

_____. *The Train Robbery Era: An Encyclopedic History.* Boulder, Colorado: Pruett Publishing Co., 1991.

_____. *Butch Cassidy: A Biography.* Lincoln, Nebraska: University of Nebraska Press, 1998.

Peak, Howard W. *A Ranger of Commerce, or 52 Years on the Road.* San Antonio, Texas: Naylor Printing Company, 1929.

Pylant, James. *Sins of the Pioneers: Crimes & Scandals in a Small Texas Town.* Stephenville, Texas: Jacobus Books, 2011.

Roberts, Oran M. *Confederate Military History of Texas.* Gulf Breeze, Florida: eBooksOnDisk.com, 2003.

Rye, Edgar. *The Quirt and the Spur: Vanishing Shadows of the Texas Frontier.* Lubbock, Texas: Texas Tech University Press, 2000.

Saunders, James Edmonds. *Early Settlers of Alabama.* Baltimore, Maryland: Genealogical Publishing Co., 2001.

Schuetz, Arden Jean and Schuetz, Wilma Jean. *People-Events and Erath County, Texas.* Stephenville, Texas: Ernie Favors, 1971-1972.

Shirley, Glenn. *The Fighting Marlows.* Fort Worth, Texas: Texas Christian University Press, 1994.

Tise, Sammy. *Texas County Sheriffs.* Albuquerque, New Mexico: Oakwood Printing, 1989.

Tyler, Ron, ed. *The New Handbook of Texas.* Austin, Texas: Texas State Historical Association, 1996.

ARTICLES

Burton, Jeff. "The Most Surprised Man in Texas," *Frontier Times*, Vol. 47, No. 2 (February-March 1973).

Clayton, Lawrence and Ledbetter, Morris. "Ledbetter Salt Works," *New Handbook of Texas*, Vol. 4, p. 138 (1996).

Favors, Ennis. "Haunted Waterhole," *Frontier Times*, Vol.47, No. 5 (August-September 1973).

Harper, Cecil, Jr. "William Lewis Cabell," *New Handbook of Texas*, Vol. 1 (1996).

Holt, R.D. "The Story of Salt in Texas," *Frontier Times*, Vol. 19, No. 10 (July 1942).

"Killing of Rube Burrows, The," *Frontier Times*, Vol. 8, No. 2 (December 1930).

Patterson, Michael. "Civil War Veterans of Northeast Tarrant County: Henderson E. Alverson," TarrantCountyTxGenWeb.

Rogers, William Warren Jr. "Rube Burrow, 'King of Outlaws,' and His Florida Adventures," *Florida Historical Quarterly*, Vol. 59, No. 2 (October 1980).

PUBLIC RECORDS

Appellate Court Opinions:
Conner v. State, 23 Tex. Ct. App. 378, 5 S.W. 189 (1887)
Houston v. State of Texas, 34 Tex. Crim. 587, 31 S.W. 403 (1895)
United States v. Hughes, 34 F. 732 (N.D. Texas 1888)

Arkansas History Commission:
Correspondence, Gov. Simon P. Hughes (1887-1888)

Erath County, Texas:
Deed Records:
Vol. J, p. 306
Vol. L, p. 568
Vol. Q, p. 262
Vol. W, p. 548
Marriage Records: Vol. D, pp. 7 and 150
State v. W.W. Cain, Cause No. 921, District Court Minutes
Tax Assessment Rolls (1886)

Lamar County, Alabama:
Deed Records:
Vol. 1, p. 460
Vol. 5, pp. 102 and 131
Vol. 9, p. 138
Vol. 13, p. 416
Vol. 15, p. 423
Estate of Reuben H. Burrow, Probate Court Records
Marriage Records (Sanford County, Alabama)

Library of Congress:
Pinkerton Detective Agency Collection

Marengo County, Alabama:
Deed Records:
Vol. Y, p. 492
Vol. 2, p. 499
Marriage Records 1883-1897, p. 314

Mississippi Department of Archives and History:
Register of Mississippi State Prisoners, Vol. E, p. 298

National Archives (Fort Worth, Texas):
Criminal Term Dockets, 1887-1910
U.S. v. Henderson Brumley et al, Cause Nos. 217, 218, 220, 249, and 409
U.S. v. Harvey Carter, Cause No. 208
U.S. v. Jim and Ben Hughes, Cause Nos. 207, 208, 212, and 404
U.S. v. John Houston et al, Cause No. 185
U.S. v. W.L. Brock et al, Cause No. 219

National Archives (Morrow, Georgia):
U.S. v. Reuben Smith, Cause No. 1002

National Archives (Washington D.C.):
Confederate Service Records
Department of Justice Correspondence (1887-1890, 1895)
Post Office Department Correspondence, Case Files of Investigators (1889-1890)
United States General Land Office Records

Ohio Historical Society:
Record of Deaths, Ohio State Penitentiary
Register of Prisoners, Ohio State Penitentiary.

Tarrant County, Texas:
Henderson Brumley v. Pacific Express Co. et al, Cause No. 4380

Texas State Library and Archives:
Adjutant General's Correspondence (1887)
Minute Men Records
Monthly Return of S.A. McMurray's Company B, Frontier Battalion, December 1886 and *June 1887*
Operations of Frontier Battalion and Report of Special Rangers From December 1, 1885, to November 30, 1892.
State of Texas v. Charles Conner, Executive Clemency File #1639

United States Census:

Benton County, Arkansas (1870)

Bienville, Louisiana (1850)

Brazos County, Texas (1870)

Buckingham County, Virginia (1860)

Callahan County, Texas (1880)

Coffee County, Alabama (1880)

Chickasaw Territory, Indian Terr. (1900)

Dale County, Alabama (1860)

Dallas County, Texas (1900)

Erath County, Texas (1860-1930)

Fayette County, Alabama (1860, 1900)

Franklin County, Georgia (1860)

Goochland County, Virginia (1870)

Hale County, Texas (1910)

Hunt County, Texas (1850, 1860)

Jefferson County, Alabama (1900-1930)

Lowndes County, Mississippi (1880)

Madison County, Mississippi (1910)

Madison County, Tennessee (1880)

Marengo County, Alabama (1880, 1900,

Marion County, Alabama (1850)

Mobile County, Alabama (1910)

Monroe County, Alabama (1860-1900)

Perry County, Alabama (1850, 1860)

Pottawatomie County, Oklahoma (1910, 1920)

Sanford County, Alabama (1870)

Shelby County, Tennessee (1900)

Stephens County, Texas (1880)

Stonewall County, Texas (1900)

Swisher County, Texas (1920)

Tallahatchie County, Mississippi (1900)

Tarrant County, Texas (1870, 1880)

Jefferson County, Texas (1930)

Johnson County, Texas (1880)
Kent County, Texas (1910)
Lamar County, Alabama
(1870-1910)

Throckmorton County, Texas
(1860)
Titus County, Texas (1850)
Upshur County, Texas (1860)
Vernon Parish, Louisiana
(1920, 1940)
Wise County, Texas (1880)

Wise County, Texas:
Deed Records:
Vol. A2, p. 265
Vol. J, p. 189

NEWSPAPERS

Alton (Illinois) Daily Telegraph
Atlanta (Georgia) Constitution
Atlanta (Georgia) Southern Expressman
Birmingham (Alabama) Age-Herald
Birmingham (Alabama) Weekly Age-Herald
Blount County (Alabama) News and Dispatch
Boston (Massachusetts) Daily Globe
Chattanooga (Tennessee) Evening Press
Cullman (Alabama) Tribune
Dallas (Texas) Morning News
Davenport (Iowa) Morning Tribune
Fort McKavett (Texas) Gazette
Fort Worth (Texas) Daily Gazette
Fort Worth (Texas) Weekly Gazette
Galveston (Texas) Daily News
Graham (Texas) Leader
Jackson (Mississippi) Daily Clarion
Linden (Alabama) Democrat Reporter
Linden (Alabama) Register
Logansport (Indiana) Daily Journal
Los Angeles (California) Herald

Memphis (Tennessee) Appeal
Memphis (Tennessee) Avalanche
Mobile (Alabama) Daily Register
Montgomery (Alabama) Advertiser
New Orleans (Louisiana) Delta
New Orleans (Louisiana) Time Picayune
New York (New York) Daily Tribune
New York (New York) Evening World
New York (New York) Sun
New York (New York) Times
New York (New York) World
Omaha (Nebraska) Daily Bee
Perrysburg (Ohio) Journal
Salt Lake (Utah) Herald
San Antonio (Texas) Daily Express
San Antonio (Texas) Daily Light
St. Paul (Minnesota) Daily Globe
Stephenville Texas) Empire
Trenton (New Jersey) Times
Vernon (Alabama) Clipper
Vernon (Alabama) Courier
Waco (Texas) Daily Examiner
Waco (Texas) Times-Herald
Washington (D.C.) Times

PRIVATE COLLECTIONS:

Erath County Criminal Case Files, Box 73, Dick Smith Library, Tarleton College, Stephenville, Texas
Green Lawn Cemetery, Columbus, Ohio (Record of Burial)

ANCESTRY.COM:

Nancy Adeline Alverson
Alabama Marriage Collection, 1880-1969
Alabama: Deaths and Burial Index, 1881-1974
Index of Vital Records for Alabama: Deaths, 1908-1959
John Thomas Burrow
Marriage Records, Marengo County, Alabama, 1883-1897
Marriage Records, Sanford County, Alabama, 1870-1877
Louisiana: Find a Grave Index, 1812-2011
Napoleon Bonapart Thornton
Oklahoma: Fine a Grave Index, 1834-2011
Texas Deaths Index, 1903-2000
Texas Marriage Collection, 1814-1900
United States General Land Office Records, 1796-1907
United States Veterans Gravesites, 1775-2006

Endnotes

Notes for the Foreword

1   Marley Brant, *Jesse James: The Man and the Myth* (New York: Berkley Books, 1998).
2   Richard Patterson, *The Train Robbery Era: An Encyclopedic History* (Boulder, CO: Pruett Publishing Co., 1991).
3   Richard Patterson, *Butch Cassidy: A Biography* (Lincoln, NE: University of Nebraska Press, 1998).
4   Rick Miller, *Sam Bass & Gang* (Austin, TX: State House Press, 1999).
5   Alvin M. Harlow, *Old Waybills: The Romance of the Express Companies* (New York: D. Appleton-Century Co., 1934), 328-331.
6   Richard Patterson, *Train Robbery: The Birth, Flowering, and Decline of a Notorious Western Enterprise. (Boulder, CO: Johnson Publishing Co., 1981), v.*
7   Philip J. Rasch (Robert K. DeArment, ed.), *Warriors of Lincoln County* (Stillwater, OK: Western Publications, 1998), ix.

Notes to Chapter One

8   *Montgomery Advertiser*, 10 October 1890; William Stanley Hoole, *The Saga of Rube Burrow* (University. Al: Confederate Publishing Co, 1981), 122.
9   www.encyclopediaofalabama.org.
10 George W. Agee, *Rube Burrow, King of Outlaws* (Chicago, Il: The Henneberry Co., 1890), 3.
11 Ibid, 6.
12 Barbara Woolbright Carruth, *Rube Burrow: Alabama Desperado* (Sulligent, Al: Ms. B's Research Service, 2007), 172.

13   *Montgomery Advertiser*, as quoted in Hoole, *Rube Burrow*, 52.

14   The 1850 U.S. Census (Marion County, Alabama) shows him to be one year old, and the 1860 U.S. Census (Perry County, Alabama) reflects that he is 11 years old.

15   *Montgomery Advertiser*, as quoted in Hoole, *Rube Burrow*, 52; 1880 U.S. Census (Lamar County, Alabama). Members of the Burrow family deny that Jasper was "feeble-minded," insisting that while he was sickly and quiet as a youth, he grew to have his own family and a successful farm. Carruth, *Rube Burrow*, 179.

16   1850 U.S. Census (Perry County, Alabama); 1870 U.S. Census (Sanford County, Alabama); 1880 U.S. Census (Wise County, Texas); Agee wrote that Rube Burrow was born in 1854. His information on the early days of the Burrow family may have come from a 12 October 1890 article in the *Atlanta Constitution*, which set out the same facts about the family as recited in Agee's book. Agee, *Rube Burrow*, 4.

17   1870 U.S. Census (Sanford County, Alabama); *Atlanta Constitution*, 12 October 1890.

18   Agee, *Rube Burrow*, 5-6.

19   *Montgomery Advertiser*, as quoted in Hoole, *Rube Burrow*, 52.

20   Agee, *Rube Burrow*, 6. The author was denied access by the Lamar County Circuit Court Clerk to circuit court records in order to verify this.

21   Agee, *Rube Burrow*, 4-5.

22   *New York Sun*, 12 October 1890.

23   *Galveston Daily News*, 9 October 1890.

24   *Trenton* [NJ] *Times*, 8 October 1890.

25   *New York Daily Tribune*, 10 November 1889.

26   *Atlanta Constitution*, 3 November 1889.

27   *Atlanta Constitution*, 12 October 1890.

28   Agee, *Rube Burrow*, 8; *Montgomery Advertiser*, as quoted in Hoole, *Rube Burrow*, 53.

29   1880 U.S. Census (Wise County, Texas); Vol. A2, p. 265; Vol. I, p. 189, Wise County, Tx, Deed Records. He had purchased forty acres in Sanford [Lamar] County, Al, in 1870. Vol. 1, p. 460, Lamar Co., Al, Deed Records. Agee mistakenly has Joel Burrow moving to Erath County, Texas. Agee, *Rube Burrow*, 8.

30   Agee, *Rube Burrow*, 9.

31 1860 U.S. Census (Fort Belknap, Throckmorton County, Texas). Virginia Alverson was born to Henderson and Sarah Alverson in Mississippi on October 4, 1853. Michael Patterson, "Civil War Veterans of Northeast Tarrant County: Henderson B. Alverson," *Tarrant County TXGenWeb.*

32 Marriage records for that year in either county do not exist. Agee, *Rube Burrow*, 9.

33 1880 U.S. Census (Wise County, Texas); *Louisiana: Find a Grave Index, 1812-2011, Ancestry,com.*

34 Virginia Catherine Alverson, *Ancestry.com.*

35 The sources all indicate that she died in 1880, but that would be impossible given the birth of her daughter in 1881. See Agee, *Rube Burrow*, 9.

36 Reward Poster, Pinkerton's National Detective Agency, 25 February 1888; Hoole, *Rube Burrow*, 7.

37 *Montgomery Advertiser*, as quoted in Hoole, *Rube Burrow*, 53.

38 Arden Jean Schuetz and Wilma Jean Schuetz, *People-Events and Erath County, Texas* (Stephenville, Tx: Ernie Favors, 1971-1972), 164-176; Ennis Favors, "Haunted Waterhole," *Frontier Times*, Vol. 47, No. 5 (Aug.-Sept. 1973).

39 *Fort Worth Daily Gazette*, 4 February 1888. Judge C.C. Cummings, who served in the Civil War in a Mississippi regiment and was shot at Gettysburg, came to Tarrant County, Texas, in January 1873 and served as County Judge from 1876 to 1880 and later as superintendent of schools. Capt. B.B. Paddock, *A Twentieth Century History and Biographical Record of North and West Texas* (Chicago, Il: The Lewis Publishing Co., 1906), Vol. 1, 206.

40 Tarrant County District Clerk to author, 23 April 2012.

41 Reward Poster, Pinkerton's National Detective Agency, 25 February 1888.

42 Carl W. Breihan, *Rube Burrow: King of the Train Robbers* (West Allis, Wi: Leather Stocking Books, 1981), 17-19.

43 Ibid; Agee, *Rube Burrow*, 9;

44 1880 U.S. Census (Lamar County, Alabama).

45 Alabama Marriage Collection, 1800-1969, *Ancestry.Com*; *Vernon [Al] Clipper*, 26 November 1880.

46 Vol. 9, p. 138, Lamar County, Alabama, Deed Records.

47 *New York Sun*, 12 October 1890.

48   1886 Erath County, Tx, Tax Assessment Rolls, p. 10.

49   Erath County Criminal Case Files, Box 73, Dick Smith Library, Tarleton College, Folders No. 440, 445, and 533, containing cases against R.D. Burrow. See also James Pylant, *Sins of the Pioneers: Crimes & Scandals in a Small Texas Town* (Stephenville, Tx: Jacobus Books, 2011), 42-43, where the two Burrows are confused.

50   Vol. D, p. 150, Erath County, Tx, Marriage Records.

51   James Abraham Hoover, *Ancestry.Com.*

52   1870 U.S. Census (Benton County, Arkansas); 1880 U.S. Census (Johnson County, Texas); *Oklahoma: Find a Grave Index, 1834-2011, Ancestry.com.*

53   *New York Sun*, 12 October 1890.

54   www.fold3.com/image/#9458270 and 8458271; Oran M. Roberts, *Confederate Military History of Texas* (Gulf Breeze, Fl: eBooksOnDisk.com, 2003), 43.

55   *Dallas Morning News*, 10 December 1938; 1850 U.S. Census (Titus County, Texas); 1870 U.S. Census (Erath County, Texas). The newspapers repeatedly referred to him as "Bromley," which all subsequent writers about Burrow and his men adopted.

56   Minute Men Records, Texas State Library, Austin, Tx.

57   1880 U.S. Census (Erath County, Texas).

58   *Fort McKavett Gazette*, Vol. 2, No. 10 (October 2003), 3; R.D. Holt, "The Story of Salt in Texas," *Frontier Times*, Vol. 19, No. 10 (July 1942), 347; Edgar Rye, *The Quirt and the Spur: Vanishing Shadows of the Texas Frontier* (Lubbock, Tx: Texas Tech University Press, 2000), 116-134; Lawrence Clayton and Morris Ledbetter, "Ledbetter Salt Works," *The New Handbook of Texas* (Ron Tyler, ed.) (Austin, Tx: Texas State Historical Assn, 1996), Vol. 4, 138.

59   1850 U.S. Census (Bienville, Louisiana); 1860 U.S. Census (Stephenville, Erath County, Texas); 1870 U.S. Census (Tarrant County, Texas); "Napoleon Bonepart Thornton," *Ancestry.com.*

60   Vol. J, p. 306; Vol. L, p. 568, Erath County, Texas, Deed Records.

61   *New York Sun*, 9 and 12 October 1890; *New York Tribune*, 10 November 1889; Agee, *Rube Burrow*, 10.

62   Patterson, *The Train Robbery Era*, 207.

63   *Birmingham Herald*, as quoted in *Vernon* [Ala] *Courier*, 3 February 1888. But see *Fort Worth Daily Gazette*, 21 December 1886, which

mentions specifically that express and mail cars were attached to the passenger cars.

64 *Fort Worth Daily Gazette*, 12 and 13 December 1886; *Galveston Daily News*, 12 December 1886; Howard W. Peak, *A Ranger of Commerce or 52 Years on the Road* (San Antonio, Tx: Naylor Printing Co., 1929), 56. On December 15, 1886, at Fort Elliott, Texas, a meeting of enlisted men adopted a resolution accusing Conner, a Tennessee native, of cowardice in allowing him and his detachment to be robbed and failing to protect their fellow passengers. He was court-martialed in February 1887, although his sentence was "remitted" in June 1890. On February 13, 1887, Conner shot to death a soldier named Blackburn at Fort Elliott, for which he was found guilty of second degree murder and sentenced to five years in the penitentiary. With the assistance of Temple Houston, son of former Texas Governor Sam Houston, Governor Sul Ross granted Conner a pardon in July 1890. *Fort Worth Daily Gazette*, 21 December 1886, and 28 July 1887; *Conner v. State, 23 Tex. Ct. App. 378; 5 S.W. 189 (1887); State of Texas v, Charles Conner*, Executive Clemency #1639, Texas State Library, Austin, Texas (Courtesy of Donaly Brice). Contemporary accounts consistently state that only three bandits held up the train. Almost all historical accounts written later inexplicably place four robbers at the scene.

65 *Fort Worth Daily Gazette*, 13 December 1886.

66 *Fort Worth Daily Gazette*, 12 December 1886.

67 *Galveston Daily News*, 12 December 1886.

68 *Operations of Frontier Battalion and Report of Special Rangers From December 1, 1885, to November 30, 1892*, Texas State Library, Austin, Texas; *Monthly Return of S.A. McMurray's Company B, Frontier Battalion, Dec. 1886*, Texas State Library, Austin, Texas; *Fort Worth Daily Gazette*, 22 December 1886.

69 S.A. McMurray to W.H. King, 3 January 1887, Texas Adjutant General's Correspondence, Texas State Library, Austin, Texas.

70 *Fort Worth Daily Gazette*, 12 December 1886.

71 *Fort Worth Daily Gazette*, 14 and 16 December 1886. See also Rick Miller, *Sam Bass & Gang* (Austin, Tx: State House Press, 1999).

72 *Dallas Morning News*, 1 February 1887.

Notes to Chapter Two

73   www.gordontexas.com.

74   1880 U.S. Census (Callahan County, Texas); Texas Muster Roll Index, 1838-1900; Texas Marriage Collection, 1814-1909; Application for Confederate Pension (January 17, 1923), *Ancestry.com.*

75   One account stated that six robbers were observed, *Galveston Daily News*, 24 January 1887, Other newspapers reported that there were eight men, *Fort Worth Daily Gazette* and *Dallas Morning News*, 24 January 1887.

76   *Fort Worth Daily Gazette*, 24 January 1887.

77   Agee, *Rube Burrow*, 12.

78   *Fort Worth Daily Gazette*, 25 January 1887.

79   *Galveston Daily News*, 24 January 1887.

80   *Fort Worth Daily Gazette*, 24 January 1887.

81   *Galveston Daily News*, 24 January 1887.

82   Ibid; *Fort Worth Daily* Gazette, 24 January 1887; *Dallas Morning News*, 24 and 26 January, 16 February 1887

83   *Dallas Morning News*, 26 January 1887. William Henry Lewis, who went by Henry, was born in Franklin County, Georgia, in 1857. His family moved first to South Carolina, then, in 1872, to Marshall, Texas. Lewis moved to Dallas in 1873. He served as a deputy tax assessor, then as a deputy sheriff for five years, being elected Dallas County Sheriff in November 1886. *Dallas Morning News*, 21 August 1888 and 11 November 1888; Sammy Tise, *Texas County Sheriffs* (Albuquerque, NM: Oakwood Printing, 1989), 146.

84   *Dallas Morning News*, 24 January 1887.

85   *Fort Worth Daily Gazette*, 24 January 1887.

86   *Dallas Morning News*, 26 January 1887.

87   *Fort Worth Daily Gazette*, 26 January 1887; *Dallas Morning News*, 2 February 1887.

88   Ibid, 27 January 1887.

89   *Dallas Morning News*, 28 January 1887.

90   *Fort Worth Daily Gazette*, 28 January 1887.

91   *Stephenville Empire*, as quoted in *Fort Worth Daily Gazette*, 5 March 1887.

92   *Dallas Morning News*, 29 January 1887.

93 Ibid, 11, 12, 13, 15, 16, 17, 18, and 19 February 1887.
94 Ibid, 19 February 1887; *Fort Worth Daily Gazette*, 19 April 1887.
95 *U.S. v. John Houston et al*, Cause No. 185, Nat'l Archives, Fort Worth, Texas; Criminal Term Dockets, 1878-1910, U.S. District Court, Northern District of Texas (Abilene/Graham), RG 21. Vol. E-48N014, Nat'l Archives, Fort Worth, Tx, p. 80; U.S. Department of Justice Files, National Archives, Washington, D.C., RG 60, No, 8447-1886.
96 Vol. W, p. 548, Deed Records, Erath County, Texas; see 1880 U.S. Census (Erath County, Texas).
97 Agee, *Rube Burrow*, 13.
98 William Lawrence Brock, *Ancestry*.com; 1860 U.S. Census (Franklin County, Georgia); 1870 U.S. Census (Brazos County, Texas).
99 Marriage Records, Erath County, Texas, Vol. D, p. 7; 1880 U.S. Census (Erath County, Texas).
100 Statement of W.L. Brock, *U.S. v. Henderson H. Brumley*, Cause No. 409, Nat'l Archives, Fort Worth, Texas; *Fort Worth Daily Gazette*, 2 February 1888.
101 Erath County, Texas, Tax Assessment Rolls (1886), p. 9.
102 Agee, *Rube Burrow*, 26.
103 Ibid, 14-15.
104 Statement of W.L. Brock, *U.S. v. Henderson H. Brumley*, Cause No. 409, Nat'l Archives, Fort Worth, Texas.
105 Ibid.
106 Ibid; Agee, *Rube Burrow*, 15-16.
107 *Fort Worth Daily Gazette*, 20 May 1887; *Galveston Daily News*, 20 May 1887. See also Jeff Burton, "The Most Surprised Man in Texas," *Frontier Times*, Vol. 47, No. 82 (Feb-March 1973), 18 et seq.
108 Statement of W.L. Brock, *U.S. v. Henderson H. Brumley*, Cause No. 409, Nat'l Archives, Fort Worth, Texas; 1880 U.S. Census (Erath County, Texas).
109 Statement of W.L. Brock, *U.S. v. Henderson H. Brumley*, Cause No. 409, Nat'l Archives, Fort Worth, Texas.
110 Ibid; *Montgomery* [Ala] *Advertiser*, 25 January 1888.
111 "Benbrook," *cityofbenbrook.com*.
112 Statement of W.L. Brock, *U.S. v. Henderson H. Brumley*, Cause No. 409, Nat'l Archives, Fort Worth, Texas.

113 *Fort Worth Daily Gazette*, 5 June 1887; *Dallas Morning* News, 15 September 1887; Statement of Richard Griffin, *U.S. v. Henderson Brumley*, Cause No. 409, Nat'l Archives, Fort Worth, Texas.

114 Statements of W.L.Brock, Richard L. Griffin, and Henderson Brumley, *U.S. v. Henderson H. Brumley*, Cause Nos. 218 and 409, Nat'l Archives, Fort Worth, Texas; Agee, *Rube Burrow*, 16-17; *Fort Worth Daily Gazette*, 5 June 1887; *Galveston Daily News*, 5 June 1887.

115 Statement of W.L. Brock, *U.S. v. Henderson H. Brumley*, Cause No. 409, Nat'l Archives, Fort Worth, Texas.

116 Murphy was subsequently arrested when identified and released on a $3000 bond, but the charge was later dropped. *Dallas Morning News*, 2 and 15 September 1887.

117 *Fort Worth Daily Gazette*, 6 June 1887; *Galveston Daily News*, 6 June 1887.

118 *Dallas Morning News*, 6 June 1887.

119 *Fort Worth Daily Gazette*, 7, 14, and 27 June 1887.

120 *Operations of Frontier Battalion and Report of Special Rangers From December 1, 1885, to November 30, 1892. P. 28; Monthly Return of S.A. McMurray's Company B, Frontier Battalion, June 1887*, Texas State L:ibrary, Austin, Texas.

121 *Fort Worth Daily Gazette*, 9 June 1887.

122 Ibid, 19 June 1887.

123 Reward notice, 2 July 1887, Adjutant General's Correspondence, Texas State Library, Austin, Texas.

124 *Fort Worth Daily Gazette*, 14 February 1888. For an accurate accounting of the Cornett-Whitley gang, see Jeff Burton, "The Most Surprised Man in Texas," *Frontier Times*, Vol. 47, No. 2 (February-March 1973), 18 et seq.

125 W.L. Cabell to A.H. Garland, 21 June 1887, RG 60, Year Files #8447-1886, Department of Justice, Nat'l Archives, Washington D.C.

126 W.L. Cabell, John Rankin, and R.B. Reagan to A.H. Garland, 4 July 1887, RG 60, Year Files #8447-1886, Department of Justice, Nat'l Archives, Washington D.C.

127 *Fort Worth Daily Gazette*, 22 June 1887.

128 T.O. Bailes to W.H. King, 24 June 1887, Adjutant General's Correspondence, Texas State Library, Austin, Texas.

129 J.A. Waldo to W. Snyder, 5 July 1887, Adjutant General's Correspondence, Texas State Library, Austin, Texas.

130 J.A. Waldo to Gov. L.S. Ross, 13 July 1887, Adjutant General's Correspondence, Texas State Library, Austin, Texas.

131 *Fort Worth Daily Gazette*, 7 July 1887.

132 Reports of Arrest, RG 60, Year Files #8447-1886, Department of Justice, Nat'l Archives, Washington D.C.; 1880 U.S. Census (Stephens County, Texas); *Dallas Morning News,*13 September 1887.

133 Charles B. Pearre was born in 1834. On November 27, 1860, he married Hallie K. Earle, who died in 1893. He was a member of Company A, Terry's Texas Rangers in the Civil War. Practicing law in Waco, Texas, in 1884 he was appointed U.S. District Attorney for the Northern District of Texas. One of his daughters married Ben Cabell, the son of William L. Cabell. In 1889 he published a scathing indictment of Reconstruction Governor E.J. Davis, entitled *A Review of the Unconstitutional Laws of the Twelfth Legislature of Texas and the Oppressions of the Present Administrations Exposed*. He died in Waco on August 11, 1908. *Waco Times-Herald*, 12 August 1908.

134 Charles B. Pearre to John E. Hollingsworth, 20 September 1887, RG 60, Year Files #8447-1886, Department of Justice, Nat'l Archives, Washington D.C.

135 Acting Postmaster General to A.H. Garland, 28 September 1887, RG 60, Year Files #8447-1886, Department of Justice, Nat'l Archives, Washington D.C.; *U.S. v. Jim and Ben Hughes*, Cause Nos. 207, 208, and 212, Criminal Term Dockets, 1879-1910, U.S. District Court, Northern District of Texas (Abilene/Graham), RG 21, Vol. E-48N014, pp. 91, 92, and 97, Nat'l Archives, Fort Worth, Texas; *Dallas Morning News*, 15, 16, and 21 September 1887.

136 *Fort Worth Daily Gazette*, 21 and 22 September 1887; *Galveston Daily News*, 21 September 1887.

137 *Fort Worth Daily Gazette*, 21 and 22 September 1887; *Galveston Daily News*, 22 September 1887.

138 *Fort Worth Daily* Gazette, 22 September 1887.

139 Ibid, 24 September 1887.

140 Ibid, 22 September 1887; *Galveston Daily News*, 22 September 1887.

141 *Fort Worth Daily Gazette*, 16 October 1887.

142 *U.S. v. John Houston*, Cause No. 185, Criminal Term Dockets, 1879-1910, U.S. District Court, Northern District of Texas, RG 21, Vol. E-48N014, p. 86, Nat'l Archives, Fort Worth, Texas; H.C. Holcombe to John E. Hollingsworth, 30 November 1887, RG 60, Year Files #8447-1886, Department of Justice, Nat'l Archives, Washington D.C. Houston was later arrested in Waller County and indicted for murder in 1895. He was found guilty and sentenced to twenty years' confinement in the state penitentiary. *Houston v. State*, 34 Tex.Crim. 587, 31 S.W. 403 (1895); *Dallas Morning News*, 5 November 1887.

143 *Waco Daily Examiner*, 5 November 1887; *Dallas Morning* News, 5 November 1887; *U.S. v. Carter*, Cause No. 208, Criminal Term Dockets. 1879-1910, U.S. District Court, Northern District of Texas, Vol. E-48N014, p. 91, Nat'l Archives, Fort Worth, Texas; H.C. Holcombe to John E. Hollingsworth, 30 November 1887, Year Files #8447-1886. Department of Justice, RG 60, Nat'l Archives, Washington D.C.

144 *U.S. v. Jim and Ben Hughes*, Cause No. 208, Criminal Term Dockets, 1879-1910, U.S. District Court, Northern District of Texas (Abilene/Graham), RG 21, Vol. E-48N014, p. 91, Nat'l Archives, Fort Worth, Texas; W.L. Cabell to A.H. Garland, 14 November 1887, RG 60, Year Files #8447-1886, Department of Justice, Nat'l Archives, Washington D.C. At the trial of the Hughes brothers, the Gordon sheriff and postmaster both testified that a man named Bob Houx had told them that he helped the brothers hold up the Gordon train along with eight other men. However, when he claimed that he could show them where the loot was buried, nothing was found and he was dismissed as a faker, then indicted for perjury. *Dallas Morning News*, 22 August 1888.

145 Agee, *Rube Burrow*, 18, 25; *Montgomery* [Ala] *Advertiser*, 25 January 1888. The account of Rube taking his children to Alabama contradicts an October 1890 account in the *New York Sun*, which stated that the children were taken to Alabama years earlier by Allen Burrow after a visit to his sons in Texas. (See Chapter One).

Notes for Chapter Three

[146] *Fort Worth Daily Gazette*, 3 February 1888.

[147] Ibid.

[148] *Fort Worth Daily Gazette*, 2 February 1888; Hoole, *Rube Burrow*, 42.

[149] Agee writes that Rube ordered the fireman to get an oil can and saturate the car, threatening to burn the messenger out. The fireman is supposed to have made an "earnest appeal" to the messenger, who then relented and opened the door. Agee, *Rube Burrow*, 20.

[150] Ibid; *Fort Worth Daily Gazette*, 11 December 1887, 2 and 3 February 1888; Agee, *Rube Burrow*, 19-20.

[151] *Galveston Daily News*, 11 December 1887; *Dallas Morning News*, 11 December 1887.

[152] *Galveston Daily* News, 11 December 1887; Fort *Worth Daily Gazette*, 3 February 1888. Agee writes that the entire posse came upon the three outlaws, allowed them to pass, and then ordered them to stop, at which time the gunfire exchange broke out. Agee, *Rube Burrow*, 21-22.

[153] *Galveston Daily News*, 11 December 1887; *Fort Worth Daily Gazette*, 11 December 1887.

[154] *Boston Daily Globe*, 28 January 1888.

[155] *Fort Worth Daily Gazette*, 11 December 1887.

[156] Telegram, Gov. Simon Hughes to Sheriff, Texarkana, 10 December 1887; telegram, Gov. Hughes to unknown person in Montgomery, Ala., 11 February 1888, *Correspondence of Gov. Simon P, Hughes, 1887-1888*, Arkansas History Commission, Little Rock, Arkansas; *Fort Worth Daily Gazette*, 11 December 1887.

[157] *Dallas Morning News*, 15 December 1887.

[158] Alvin F. Harlow, *Old Waybills: The Romance of the Express Companies* (New York, NY: D. Appleton-Century Co., 1934), 288.

[159] Ibid, 342.

[160] James D. Horan, *The Pinkertons: The Detective Dynasty That Made History* (New York, NY: Crown Publishers, Inc., 1967), 371; Agee, *Rube Burrow*, 21.

[161] *Dallas Morning News*, 25 December 1887; Boston *Daily Globe*, 28 January 1888; *Montgomery Advertiser*, 25 January 1888.

162 Agee, *Rube Burrow*, 22-24; *Boston Daily Globe*, 28 January 1888.

163 *Dallas Morning News*, 2 January 1888.

164 Agee, *Rube Burrow*, 22-24; *Boston Daily Globe*, 28 January 1888.

165 *Fort Worth Daily Gazette*, 1 and 3 January 1888; *Dallas Morning News*, 1 January 1888; Boston *Daily Globe*, 28 January 1888.

166 One possible candidate is Archie W. Jerry, who lived in neighboring Fayette County in 1900. U.S. Census 1900 (Fayette County, Alabama).

167 Agee, *Rube Burrow*, 27-30; *Vernon* [Ala] *Courier*, 13 January 1888; *Birmingham Age-Herald*, 16 January 1888, courtesy Barbara Carruth, Sulligent, Alabama; Hoole, *Rube Burrow*, 53.

168 Agee, *Rube Burrow*, 29-30; *Boston Daily Globe*, 28 January 1888.

169 *Montgomery* [Ala] *Advertiser*, 23 January 1888 and 18 August 1909. Callahan later changed his story and claimed that he compared the two men with photographs of Rube and Jim, concluding they were the wanted robbers. As he was writing the message to be telegraphed to the Montgomery police, he said, they came up behind him and put a pistol to his head. He was then able to slip the message to a boy to take to the telegraph office. He said that the two men watched him at every stop to make sure he did not send any telegrams. *Birmingham Age-Herald*, 1 February 1888, as quoted in *Vernon* [Ala] *Courier*, 3 February 1888.

170 Agee, *Rube Burrow*, 31-32; *Montgomery* [Ala] *Advertiser*, 23 January 1888.

171 Ibid.

172 *Montgomery* [Ala] *Advertiser*, 23 January 1888.

173 Ibid, 24 January 1888.

174 Ibid.

175 Agee, *Rube Burrow*, 36.

176 Ibid, 36-37.

177 *U.S. v. Jim and Ben Hughes and Harvey Carter*, Cause No. 404, Minutes, U.S. District Court, Northern District of Texas (Dallas), RG 21, Vol. E-48N028, p. 349-350, Nat'l Archives, Fort Worth, Texas; *Fort Worth Daily Gazette*, 26 January 1888; *Dallas Morning News*, 26 January 1888.

178 *Montgomery* [Ala] *Advertiser*, 26 January 1888.

179 Ibid.

180 Ibid, 27 January 1888; *Fort Worth Daily Gazette*, 29 January 1888.

181 Agee, *Rube Burrow*, 33; *Birmingham Age-Herald*, 1 February 1888, as quoted in *Vernon* [Ala] *Courier*, 3 February 1888.

182 *Dallas Morning News*, 28 and 29 January 1888; *Fort Worth Daily Gazette*, 27 and 28 January 1888.

183 *Fort Worth Daily Gazette*, 29 January 1888.

184 Born in Kentucky in 1844, Judge Robert E. Beckham served in the Confederate cavalry, and began the practice of law in 1866. He moved to Fort Worth in 1872 and in 1878 was elected mayor. He was elected Tarrant County Judge in 1880, and as District Judge in 1884. He retired in 1892 and resumed his law practice. Capt. B.B. Paddock, ed. *A Twentieth Century History and Biographical Record of North and West Texas* (Chicago, Il: The Lewis Publishing Co., 1906), Vol. 2, p. 196.

185 *Dallas Morning News*, 29 January 1888.

186 *Henderson Brumley v. Pacific Express Company et al*, Cause No. 4380, 17th Judicial District Court, Tarrant County, Texas; *Dallas Morning News*, 31 January 1888.

187 *Fort Worth Daily Gazette*, 29 January 1888; *Henderson Brumley v. Pacific Express Co. et al*, Cause No. 4380. 17th Judicial District Court, Tarrant County, Texas.

188 *Henderson Brumley v. Pacific Express Company et al*, Cause No. 4380, Minutes, 17th Judicial District Court, Tarrant County, Texas, Vol. O, p. 26.

189 *Dallas Morning News*, 31 January 1888; *Stephenville* [Tex] *Empire*, 4 February 1888.

190 *San Antonio Daily Express*, 31 January 1888; *Galveston Daily News*, 31 January 1888; *Fort Worth Daily Gazette*, 2 February 1888; *Dallas Morning News*, 7 February 1888.

191 *Fort Worth Daily Gazette*, 2 and 3 February 1888; *Dallas Morning News*, 3 February 1888; *Galveston Daily News*, 3 February 1888.

192 *Dallas Morning News*, 4 February 1888.

193 *Vernon* [Ala] *Courier*, 17 February 1888.

194 *Fort Worth Daily Gazette*, 5 February 1888.

195 *Dallas Morning News*, 14, 17, and 18 February 1888.

196 *Galveston Daily News*, 23 February 1888; *Fort Worth Daily Gazette*, 23 February 1888.

197 Reward Poster, 25 February 1888, Pinkerton National Detective Agency, Library of Congress, Washington D.C.

198 *New York Times*, 1 March 1888; *Fort Worth Weekly Gazette*, 2 March 1888.

199 *U.S. v. Henderson Brumley et al*, Cause No. 217. U.S. District Court, Northern District of Texas (Abilene/Graham), Nat'l Archives, Fort Worth, Texas.

200 *U.S. v. Henderson Brumley*, Cause No. 220 (409), U.S. District Court, Northern District of Texas (Abilene/Graham), Nat'l Archives, Fort Worth, Texas.

201 *U.S. v. W.L. Brock et al*, Cause No. 219 (408), U.S. District Court, Northern District of Texas (Abilene/Graham), Nat'l Archives, Fort Worth, Texas.

202 *U.S. v. Hughes*, 34 F. 732 (N.D. Texas 1888); *U.S. v. Hughes*, Cause No. 207, Criminal Term Dockets, 1879-1910; U.S. District Court, Northern District of Texas, RG 21, Vol. E-48N014, p. 97, Nat'l Archives, Fort Worth, Texas.

203 *Dallas Morning News*, 25 March 1888.

204 Hoole, *Rube Burrow*, 52.

205 Ibid, 54.

206 *Vernon [Al] Courier*, 13 April 1888.

Notes for Chapter Four

207 Agee, *Rube Burrow*, 133.

208 *Dallas Morning News*, 18 July 1890.

209 Leonard Calvert Brock was born July 13, 1860, in Coffee County, Alabama, to Dr. Joseph E. Brock and Sallie F. Harrell Brock, who had married in Georgia before moving to Elba, Alabama. Unmarried, Brock received a very limited education and worked on his parents' farm until he went to Texas in 1886 because of involvement in a "cutting scrape" with an African-American and an accusation of killing another man. In Texas, he worked various jobs centered around cattle both in Texas and the Indian Territory. Agee, *Rube Burrow*, 107-108; 1860 U.S. Census Newton, Dale County, Alabama); 1880 U.S. Census (Coffee County, Alabama).

210 Agee, *Rube Burrow*, 40, 109-111.

211 Ibid, 47.

212 Ibid, 44, 46, 112-114,

213   Ibid, 39.

214   *Fort Worth Daily Gazette*, 6 May 1888; *Dallas Morning News*, 7 and 8 May 1888; *U.S. v. Brumley*, Cause No. 409 (220), U.S. District Court, Northern District of Texas, Nat'l Archives, Fort Worth, Texas.

215   *Dallas Morning News*, 28 and 31 May, 1 June 1888.

216   *U.S. v. Henderson Brumley*, Cause No. 409, Minutes, U.S. District Court, Northern District of Texas (Dallas), RG 21, Vol. 2 (E-48N028), p. 384.

217   Ibid, p. 385; *Galveston Daily News*, 7 June 1888.

218   *San Antonio Daily Light*, 12 June 1888.

219   *San Antonio Daily Express*, 12 June 1888; *Fort Worth Daily Gazette* 12 June 1888.

220   *Galveston Daily News*, 20 July 1888.

221   *U.S. v. Henderson Brumley et al*, Cause No. 249, U.S. District Court, Northern District of Texas (Abilene/Graham), Nat'l Archives, Fort Worth, Texas.

222   *Galveston Daily News*, 3 August 1888.

223   *Galveston Daily News*, 12 September 1888.

224   Agee, *Rube Burrow*, 49-50.

225   Ibid, 51; *San Antonio Daily Express*, 10 October 1888; *St. Paul* [Mn] *Daily Globe*, 1 August 1889.

226   *Fort Worth Daily Gazette*, 13 and 14 December 1888.

227   Ibid, 18 December 1888.

228   Charles B. Pearre to W.H.H. Miller, 19 December 1888, RG 60, Central Files, U.S. Department of Justice, No. 10,034, Nat'l Archives, Washington D.C.

229   Carroll County, Mississippi. MSGenWeb Project online. In 1937 the town was the site of an horrific lynching by a mob of two black men accused of murder.

230   1880 U.S. Census (Jackson, Madison County, Tennessee).

231   Agee, *Rube Burrow*, 114-116; *Memphis* [Tn] *Avalanche*, 17 December 1888; *New York Daily Tribune*, 17 December 1888; *Alton* [Illinois] *Daily Telegraph*, 18 December 1888; Agee, *Rube Burrow*, 53-54; *Memphis* Appeal, 17 December 1888; Memphis *Appeal*, 18 December 1888, as quoted in Hoole, *Rube Burrow*, 62.

232   *Memphis Appeal*, 19, 20, and 21 December 1888, as quoted in Hoole, *Rube Burrow*, 60, 63-64.

233 *Memphis Appeal*, 18 December 1888.

234 Rick Miller, *The Train Robbing Bunch* (College Station, Tx: Creative Publishing Co., 1983), 81-87. Eugene Franklin Bunch was born on February 9, 1843, in Noxubee County, Mississippi. He served from 1861 to 1863 in the Fourth Louisiana Regiment, being surrendered at Port Hudson in July 1863. He taught school in Tangipahoa Parish, Louisiana, marrying Flavia H. Flynn on December 22, 1869. Bunch and his wife moved to Cooke County, Texas, in the early 1870s, where he again taught school, then served as County Clerk from 1876 to 1882. In 1885 he briefly edited a newspaper and sold real estate in Wichita Falls. A not-very-successful gambler, he abandoned his family about 1887 and moved with a girlfriend, Cora Littlehale, to New Orleans, and with the assistance of J. Leon Pounds, executed the November 1888 robbery.

235 Agee, *Rube Burrow*, 58.

236 Ibid, 60, 116-119.

237 Ibid, 61.

238 *New York Sun*, 12 October 1890; Horan, *The Pinkertons*, 372.

239 Carl Carmer, *The Fine Art of Robbery* (New York: Grossett & Dunlap, 1966), 102.

240 *U.S. v. Henderson Brumley*, Cause No. 409, U.S. District Court, Northern District of Texas, Nat'l Archives, Fort Worth, Texas.

241 *U.S. v. Henderson Brumley, Cause No. 409*, Minutes, U.S. District Court, Northern District of Texas, RG 21, Vol. 2, E-48N028, p. 447, Nat'l Archives, Fort Worth, Texas; *Dallas Morning News*, 5, 6, and 7 February 1889; *Fort Worth Daily Gazette*, 7 February 1889.

242 *U.S. v. Henderson Brumley et al*, Cause No. 217, Criminal Term Dockets, 1879-1910. U.S. District Court, Northern District of Texas (Abilene/Graham), RG 21, Vol. E-48N014, p. 121; Glenn Shirley, *The Fighting Marlows* (Fort Worth, Tx: Texas Christian University Press, 1994), 91-92; *Graham* [Tx] *Leader*, 28 March 1889.

243 W.L. Cabell to U.S. Attorney General, 29 April 1889, RG 60, Dept. of Justice, Year Files #3972-1889, Nat'l Archives, Washington D.C.

244 *U.S. v. W.L. Brock et al*, Cause No. 408, Minutes, U.S. District Court, Northern District of Texas (Dallas), RG 21, Vol. 2, E-48N028, pp. 490-491, Nat'l Archives, Fort Worth, Texas; *Galveston Daily News*, 29 May 1889.

245 See *State v. W.W. Cain*, Cause No. 921, District Court Minutes, Erath County, Texas. Cain had been charged with carrying a pistol, but the case was dismissed on April 9, 1884, because he was a "civil officer" in the discharge of his official duties at the time of his arrest. Diligent research has failed to determine what office he held. His 51-year-old widow can be found in the 1900 Stephenville, Erath County, Census.

246 Vol. 13, p. 416, Deed Records, Lamar County, Alabama.

247 Agee, *Rube Burrow*, 63-66, 119-120; *Vernon [Ala] Courier*, 18 July 1889; *New York Sun*, 19 July 1889; *Galveston Daily News*, 19 July 1889. *Atlanta Constitution*, 3 November 1889. It should be noted that a niece of Rube Burrow, Evie Hankins Livingston, in 1986, at the age of 90, in an effort to "set the record straight," pointed out that a number of men in the area resembled Rube, the lighting was poor, and Rube was in Texas at the time, she stating that her mother had received a letter from Rube postmarked only a few days before the killing. Mrs. Livingston also opined that it could have been "Joe Jackson" who shot Graves. Carruth, *Rube Burrow*, 175-178. In another account, the man who shot Graves was masked, but Graves recognized him as Rube Burrow. Joe Acee, *Rube Burrows: Alabama's Most Famous Train Robber* (Vernon, Al: The Vernon Democrat, 1989), 75-76.

248 Agee, *Rube Burrow*, 121.

249 Ibid, 66; *New York Evening World*, 31 July 1889.

250 *Vernon [Ala] Courier*, 1 August 1889.

251 *Atlanta Constitution*, 3 November 1889; *New York Sun*, 12 October 1890.

252 *New York Sun*, 30 July 1889.

253 *Boston Daily Globe*, 31 July 1889; *New York Tribune*, 31 July 1889.

254 *Vernon [Ala] Courier*, 1 August 1889.

255 *New York Evening World*, 31 July 1889.

256 *St. Paul [Mn] Daily Globe*, 1 August 1889.

257 *Vernon [Ala] Courier*, 1 August 1889; *Birmingham Age-Herald*, as quoted in Hoole, *Rube Burrow*, 76-77.

258 *Birmingham Age-Herald*, as quoted in Hoole, *Rube Burrow*, 77.

259 *Vernon [Ala] Courier*, 8 August 1889.

260 Ibid.

261 Ibid, 19 September 1889.

262 *Fort Worth Daily Gazette*, 31 August 1889.

263 Agee, *Rube Burrow*, 68.

264 Ibid, 69; 1870 U.S. Census (Vernon and Moscow, Lamar County, Alabama).

265 Register of Prisoners, Ohio State Penitentiary, Ohio Historical Society, 370-372; Vol. E, p. 298, Register of Mississippi State Prisoners, Mississippi Department of Archives and History.

266 Agee, *Rube Burrow*, 69-70, 123.

267 Ibid, 70-71, 123-124.

268 Ibid, 71-74, 124-125.

Notes for Chapter Five

269 Agee, *Rube Burrow*, 74-79, 125-127; *Birmingham Weekly Age-Herald*, 2 October 1889, as quoted in Breihan, *Rube Burrow*, 79-83; *New York Tribune*, 26 September 1889; *Galveston Daily News*, 26 September 1889. Some news accounts stated that the mail agent had tried to hide the registered packages in the adjoining baggage car, but was intercepted by the robbers.

270 *Birmingham Weekly Age-Herald*, as quoted in Breihan, *Rube Burrow*, 81.

271 *New York Tribune*, 26 September 1889.

272 J.C. Clarke to A.G. Sharpe, 27 September 1889, Case Files of Investigators, Records of Post Office, RG 28, Nat'l Archives, Washington D,C.

273 *Logansport* [In] *Daily Journal*, 28 September 1889.

274 Agee, *Rube Burrow*, 81, 127.

275 G.W. Agee to A.G. Sharp, 8 October 1889, Case Files of Investigators, Records of Post Office, RG 28, Nat'l Archives, Washington D.C.

276 Agee, *Rube Burrow*, 91.

277 *Atlanta Constitution*, 29 October 1889.

278 Ibid, 29 and 31 October, 1889; *Blount County News and* Dispatch, 31 October 1889, courtesy of Barbara Carruth; *Covington* {Al] *Times*, 2 November 1889; C.R. Clark to A.G. Sharp, 29 October 1889, Case Files of Investigators, Records of Post Office, RG 28, Nat'l Archives, Washington D.C.

279 *Blount County News and Dispatch*, 7 November 1889, quoted in Carruth, *Rube Burrow*, 67; *Cullman* [Al] *Tribune*, 21 November 1889.

280 *Vernon* {Al] *Courier*, 31 October 1889.

281 *Atlanta Constitution*, 3 November 1889.

282 Ibid.

283 *New York Daily Tribune*, 10 November 1889.

284 Agee, *Rube Burrow*, 92.

285 *Atlanta Constitution*, 9 November 1889.

286 *Boston Daily Globe*, 10 November 1889; Agee, *Rube Burrow*, 92-93; Hoole, *Rube Burrow*, 92.

287 *Boston Daily Globe*, 10 November 1889.

288 *Vernon* {Al] *Courier*, 14 and 28 November 1889; Hoole, *Rube Burrow*, 92-95.

289 *Vernon* [Al] *Courier*, 21 November 1889.

290 *New Orleans Times-Democrat*, 23 August 1892; *New Orleans Delta*, 23 August 1892, quoted in Zuma F. Magee, ed., *The Eugene F. Bunch Story (Franklinton, La: Zuma F. Magee, 1975), 32-41.*

291 Agee, *Rube Burrow*, 82-88.

292 *Montgomery Advertiser*, as quoted in Hoole, *Rube Burrow*, 98; *St. Paul* [Mn] *Daily Globe*, 15 December 1889.

293 Agee, *Rube Burrow*, 90.

294 *New York Sun*, 19 December 1889; *Cullman* [Al] *Tribune*, 19 December 1889.

295 Agee, *Rube Burrow*, 137.

296 Ibid, 90.

297 *Atlanta Constitution*, 6 April 1890.

298 Agee, *Rube* Burrow, 93.

299 *New York Sun*, 26 January 1890.

300 *Salt Lake* [Ut] *Herald*, 1 March 1890.

301 Agee, *Rube Burrow*, 93-94, 128-129; William Warren Rogers, Jr., "Rube Burrow, 'King of Outlaws,' and his Florida Adventures," *Florida Historical Quarterly*, Vol. 59, No. 2 (Oct. 1980), 185.

302 Agee, *Rube Burrow*, 95-96, 129, 131.

303 Rogers, "Rube Burrow," 184.

304 Ibid; Agee, *Rube Burrow*, 96-97. The name of the ferry owner could also have been "Broxton." In 1885, W.H. Broxton was a farmer in Santa Rosa County with a 13-year-old son, William. Also in the

county was a laborer, J.R. Broxton, who had a 10-year-old son named William. 1885 Florida Census (Santa Rosa County),

305 Rogers, "Rube Burrow," 185.
306 Agee, *Rube Burrow*, 95-96.
307 Ibid, 96-97.
308 Ibid, 98-102; Rogers, "Rube Burrow," 186-189.
309 *Atlanta Constitution*, 9 February 1890.
310 The 1880 census lists a James H. Wells, 49, with his wife, Elizabeth, 31, and five children, including three daughters. 1880 Census (Santa Rosa County, Florida).
311 Agee, *Rube Burrow*, 142-144; Rogers, "Rube Burrow," 189-190.
312 *New York Sun*, 12 November 1890.
313 *Vernon Courier*, 13 March 1890.
314 Rogers, "Rube Burrow," 190.
315 *St. Paul* [Mn] *Daily Globe*, 12 April 1890.
316 *Vernon Courier*, 17 April 1890.
317 G.W. Agee to A.G. Sharpe, 14 April 1890, Case Files of Investigators, Sep-Oct 1889, Records of Post Office, RG 28, Nat'l Archives, Washington D.C.; *St. Paul* [Mn] *Daily Globe*, 12 April 1890.
318 Alonzo G. Sharp to E.G. Rathbone, 15 April 1890; and E.G. Rathbone to George A. Dice, 26 April 1890, Case Files of Investigators, Sep-Oct 1889, Records of Post Office, RG 28, Nat'l Archives, Washington D.C.
319 Agee, *Rube Burrow*, 137.
320 *U.S. v. Reuben Smith*, Cause No. 1002, Court Minutes, pp. 264, 405-406, Federal District Court, Southern District of Mississippi, Jackson, Mississippi, Nat'l Archives, Morrow, Georgia.
321 Ibid, pp. 312-317, 407-408.
322 Ibid, p. 317.
323 G.W. Agee to A.G. Sharp, 24 July 1890, Letters Received Year Files #8891-1890, Department of Justice, RG 60, Nat'l Archives, Washington D.C.
324 *Atlanta Constitution*, 5 June 1890.
325 *Trenton* [NJ] *Times*, 11 June 1890.
326 Agee, *Rube Burrow*, 130-131.
327 Ibid, 132.

328 Ibid, 105-106; *Vernon Courier*, 17 and 24 July 1890; *Dallas Morning News*, 18 July 1890. The Pinkertons later tried to take credit for Brock's arrest. Horan, *The Pinkertons*, 374.

Notes for Chapter Six

329 *Atlanta Constitution*, 17 July 1890.

330 *Galveston Daily News*, 20 July 1890; *Dallas Morning News*, 18 July 1890.

331 Agee, *Rube Burrow*, 106.

332 Ibid, 135; *Atlanta Constitution*, 24 November 1890.

333 Agee, *Rube Burrow*, 132-133.

334 Telegram, A.G. Sharp, Chattanooga, TN, to E.G. Rathbone, Washington D.C., 22 July 1890, Records of Post Office, RG 28, Nat'l Archives, Washington D.C.; *Daily Clarion-Ledger* [Jackson, Ms], 24 July 1890.

335 J.W. Wanamaker to W.H.H. Miller, 2 September 1890, Letters Received Year Files #8891-1890, Department of Justice, RG 60, Nat'l Archives, Washington D.C.

336 Agee, *Rube Burrow*, 178.

337 Ibid, 138-141.

338 Ibid, 139.

339 Ibid, 141; *Atlanta Constitution*, 24 November 1890.

340 Agee, *Rube* Burrow, 144-146; Rogers, "Rube Burrow," 191.

341 *Atlanta Constitution*, 3 September 1890; Agee, *Rube Burrow*, 146-150; Rogers, "Rube Burrow," 192-193; Hoole, *Rube Burrow*, 108-110.

342 Agee, *Rube Burrow*, 150.

343 Hoole, *Rube Burrow*, 110-111.

344 Rogers, "Rube Burrow," 195.

345 *Atlanta Constitution*, 5 and 7 September 1890.

346 *San Antonio Daily Light*, 20 September 1890.

347 Agee, *Rube* Burrow, 152-153. Rogers' account has the detectives spotting Burrow in the cabin eating with the Wells family. Suddenly, two of Wells' sons were supposed to have come out of the cabin cracking ox whips, which the concealed detectives thought was gunfire. The cabin was rushed by the detectives, only

to have Burrow escape into the surrounding swamp. Rogers, "Rube Burrow," 196-197.

348 Rogers, "Rube Burrow," 197; *Atlanta Constitution*, 21 September 1890; Agee, *Rube Burrow*, 152-153.

349 Agee, *Rube Burrow*, 154-155.

350 *Montgomery Advertiser*, 10 October 1890.

351 Ibid, 156.

352 1880 U.S. Census (Bell's Landing, Monroe County, Alabama); *Montgomery Journal*, as quoted in *Kansas City Times*, 6 November 1890.

353 *Linden [Al] Register*, 10 October 1890. McDuffie was reported to have previously been severely cut with a knife in the stomach, causing him to shoot his assailant. When the local sheriff asked him if the man was dead, his response was, "Slightly." *Montgomery Journal*, as quoted in *Kansas City Times*, 6 November 1890.

354 Agee, *Rube Burrow*. 157-158.

355 Ibid, 158.

356 Ibid, 158-159.

357 1900 U.S. Census (Marengo County, Alabama); Vol. Y, p. 492 and Vol. 2, p. 499, Deed Records, Marengo County, Alabama; Agee, *Rube Burrow*, 171.

358 Agee, *Rube* Burrow, 159-160.

359 Ibid, 160; 1880 U.S. Census (Marengo County, Alabama).

360 Agee, *Rube Burrow*, 160.

361 While there is no present-day Blue Lick in Alabama, there was a Blue Lick Cemetery in Franklin County, to the north of Lamar County in far northwestern Alabama, located at the present-day Cedar Creek Reservoir.

362 *Linden [Al] Democrat Reporter*, 11 February 1982, as quoted in Carruth, *Rube Burrow*, 165-167.

363 Agee, *Rube Burrow*, 160-161; *Vernon Courier*, 16 October 1890.

364 *Mobile Daily Register*, 8 October 1890; *Montgomery Advertiser*, 8 October 1890.

365 Agee, *Rube Burrow*, 162; *Vernon Courier*, 16 October 1890.

366 *Linden [Al] Democrat Reporter*, 11 February 1982, as quoted in Carruth, *Rube Burrow*, 165-167.

367 *Montgomery Advertiser*, 8 and 9 October, 1890.

368 Agee, *Rube Burrow*, 163-166; *Vernon Courier*, 16 October 1890.

Notes for Chapter Seven

369 *Montgomery Advertiser*, 10 October 1890.
370 Ibid.
371 *New Orleans Times-Picayune*, 18 October 1890. Carter was later quoted as saying that Burrow started to say, "I am Rube Burrow, a free man, and I intend to kill—" when both began shooting. *Southern Expressman* [Atlanta, Ga.], unknown date in April 1891.
372 *New York Sun*, 12 September 1891.
373 Agee, *Rube Burrow*, 166-169; *Linden* [Al] *Reporter*, 10 October 1890; Joel D. Jones, "Jail Rube Burrows in Linden," *Linden Democrat Reporter*, 11 February 1982, as quoted in Carruth, *Rube Burrow*, 166-170.
374 *Linden* [Al] *Reporter*, 10 October 1890; Agee, *Rube Burrow*, 173; *Birmingham Age-Herald*, 13 October 1890.
375 Agee, *Rube Burrow*, 172.
376 *Montgomery Advertiser*, 9 October 1890.
377 Ibid, 10 October 1890.
378 Ibid, 9 October 1890.
379 Ibid, 10 October 1890; "The Killing of Rube Burrows," *Frontier Times*, Vol. 8, No. 2 (December 1930), 109-110.
380 *Chattanooga Evening Press*, 16 October 1890.
381 Acee, *Rube Burrows*, 108.
382 *Atlanta Constitution*, 12 October 1890.
383 Agee, *Rube Burrow*, 173-175.
384 *Montgomery Advertiser*, 10 October 1890.
385 *Atlanta Constitution* as quoted in *Dallas Morning News*, 6 September 1891.
386 *Birmingham Age-Herald*, 12 October 1890.
387 Ibid, 13 October 1890.
388 *Davenport* [Iowa] *Morning Tribune*, 14 October 1890; *Los Angeles* [Ca] *Herald*, 7 November 1890.
389 *Vernon Courier*, 16 October 1890.
390 Ibid, 23 October 1890.
391 *New York World*, 12 November 1890.
392 *Atlanta Constitution*, 24 November 1890.
393 *Vernon Courier*, 15 January 1891.
394 Acee, *Rube Burrows*, 109.

395 Agee, *Rube Burrow*, 171-172.
396 *Vernon Courier*, 23 October 1890.
397 *Atlanta Constitution*, 24 November 1890.
398 Agee, *Rube Burrow*, 191-192; see also Vol. 15, p. 423, Deed Records, Lamar County, Alabama, wherein $1,600 is shown to have been received by Allen Burrow and his wife from R.H. Burrow shortly after the Duck Hill robbery.
399 *Linden Reporter*, 31 October and 7 November, 1890.
400 Hoole, *Rube Burrow*, 139; *Southern Expressman* [Atlanta, Ga], April 1891.
401 *Southern Expressman* [Atlanta, Ga.], April 1891.
402 *Vernon Courier*, 30 October 1890.
403 J.W. Wanamaker to W.H.H. Miller, 2 September 1890, Letters Received Files #8891-1890, Department of Justice Files, RG 60, Nat'l Archives, Washington D.C.
404 Agee, *Rube Burrow*, 178-179.
405 Ibid, 180-181.
406 Ibid, 181-184; *Daily Clarion-Ledger* [Jackson, Ms], 10 November 1890; *Atlanta Constitution*, 11 November 1890.
407 *Atlanta Constitution*, 24 November 1890.
408 Agee, *Rube Burrow*, 185-186.
409 *Galveston Daily News*, 15 November 1890.
410 *Daily Clarion-Ledger* [Jackson, Ms], 19 November 1890.
411 Agee, *Rube Burrow*, 189-190.
412 *Fort Worth Daily Gazette*, 15 November 1890;
413 *San Antonio Daily Light*, 20 November 1890.
414 *Daily Clarion-Ledger* [Jackson, Ms], 8 December 1890.
415 Register of Prisoners, Ohio State Penitentiary, Ohio Historical Society, 370-372.

Notes for Chapter Eight

416 *Vernon Courier*, 22 January 1891.
417 *Fort Worth Daily Gazette*, 21 December 1891.
418 *Montgomery Advertiser*, 10 October 1890.
419 *Vernon Courier*, 22 January 1891.
420 *New York Sun*, 12 September 1891.

421 Ibid, 25 December 1890.
422 Unknown newspaper article, 28 October 1891, courtesy of Barbara Carruth.
423 *New York Sun*, 12 September 1891; *St. Paul* [Mn] *Daily Globe*, 12 September 1891. It was later asserted incorrectly that Carter received all of the reward offered by the Post Office Department. Marshall Cushing, *The Story of Our Post Office: The Greatest Government Department in all its Phases* (Boston, Ma: A.M. Thayer & Co., 1893), 654-656.
424 E.G. Rathbone to Jefferson D. Carter, 10 September 1891, as quoted In Carruth, *Rube Burrow*, 196-197.
425 *Galveston Daily News*, 21 November 1891.
426 *Dallas Morning News*, 21 September 1891.
427 *Omaha* [Ne] *Daily Bee*, 30 December 1891; unknown newspaper clipping quoted in Carruth, *Rube Burrow*, 87-88.
428 *Estate of* Reuben *H. Burrow*, Probate Court, Lamar County, Alabama.
429 *Washington* [D.C.] *Times*, 10 March 1895; *Perrysburg* [Oh] *Journal*, 16 March 1895. The author was denied access to the Lamar County circuit court records by the circuit court clerk to confirm this information.
430 Vol. 15, p. 423, Deed Records, Lamar County, Alabama.
431 *Express Gazette*, Vol. 20, No. 5 (May 15, 1895), 108.
432 Ibid; S.A. Sternberger to U.S. Attorney General, 23 April 1895, Letters Received Year Files #8891-1890, Department of Justice, RG 60, Nat'l Archives, Washington D.C.; Record of Deaths, Ohio State Penitentiary, 352-353, Ohio Historical Society.
433 "Rohben Smith," Record of Burial, Green Lawn Cemetery, Columbus, Ohio,
434 James Edmonds Saunders, *Early Settlers of Alabama* (Baltimore, Md: Genealogical Publishing Co., 2001), 358; 1860 U.S. Census(Buckingham County, Virginia); 1870 U.S. Census (Goochland County, Virginia); 1900 U.S. Census (Shelby County, Tennessee); Agee Lineage, Ancestry.com.
435 Michael Patterson, "Civil War Veterans of Northeast Tarrant County: Henderson B. Alverson," *Tarrant County TXGenWeb*; 1860 U.S. Census (Ft. Belknap, Throckmorton County, Texas); 1870 and 1880 U.S. Census (Tarrant County, Texas).

436 1850 and 1860 U.S. Census (Hunt County, Texas); 1880 U.S. Census (Callahan County, Texas); 1900 U.S. Census (Stonewall County, Texas); 1910 U.S. Census (Jayton, Kent County, Texas); 1920 U.S. Census (Kress Village, Swisher County, Texas); Texas Marriage Collection, 1814-1909, *Ancestry.com.*; Texas Muster Roll Index, 1838-1900, *Ancestry.com.*; Application for Confederate Pension, *Ancestry.com*; Texas Death Index, 1903-2000, *Ancestry.com.*

437 1900, 1910, ad 1930 U.S. Census (Birmingham, Jefferson County, Alabama); Index of Vital Records for Alabama: Deaths, 1908-1959, Certificate #11559, *Ancestry.com*; *Alabama, Deaths and Burial Index, 1881-1974*(Provo, Ut: Ancestry.com Operations, Inc., 2011), film no. 1908510.

438 Texas Marriage Collection, 1814-1909, Ancestry.com.

439 1860 U.S. Census (Franklin County, Georgia); 1870 U.S. Census (Bryan, Brazos County, Texas); 1900 U.S. Census (Dallas County, Texas); 1910 U.S. Census (Plainview, Hale County, Texas); 1920 U.S. Census (Amarillo, Potter County, Texas); Texas Death Index, 1903-2000, *Ancestry.com;* Vol. D, p. 7, Marriage Records, Erath County, Texas; Erath County, Texas, Tax Assessment Rolls (1886), p. 9.

440 1850 U.S. Census (Titus County, Texas); 1860 U.S. Census (Hunt County, Texas); 1870, 1880, 1920, and 1930 U.S. Census (Erath County, Texas); Minute Men Records, Texas State Library, Austin, Texas; Confederate Service Records, Nat'l Archives, Washington D.C.; *Dallas Morning News*, 20 July 1915 and 10 December 1938.

441 1860 U.S. Census (Gilmer, Upshur County, Texas); 1870 U.S. Census (Osage Township, Benton County, Arkansas); 1880 U.S. Census (Alvarado, Johnson County, Texas); 1900 U.S. Census (Chickasaw Territory, Indian Territory); 1910 and 1920 U.S. Census (Pottawatomie County, Oklahoma); Oklahoma, Find a Grave Index, 1834-2011, *Ancestry.com.*

442 1860 U.S. Census (Perry County, Alabama); 1870 and 1880 U.S. Census (Lamar County, Alabama); Agee, *Rube Burrow*, 3-4.

443 1866 Fayette County, Alabama State Census; 1870 U.S. Census (Lawrence, Sanford County, Alabama); 1880 U.S. Census (Wise County, Texas); Vol. A2, p. 265 and Vol. J, p. 189, Deed Records, Wise County, Texas; U.S. General Land Office Records, 1796-1907; Vol. 1, p. 460, Deed Records, Dallas (Lamar) County, Alabama; U.S. Veterans Gravesites, ca. 1775-2006, *Ancestry.com.*

444 John Thomas Burrow, *Ancestry.com*; 1880 U.S. Census (Lamar County, Alabama); Vol. 5, p. 102 & 131; Vol. 13, p. 416; and Vol. 15, p. 423, Deed Records, Lamar County, Alabama; Marriage Records, Sanford County, Alabama, 1870-1877, *Ancestry. Com.*

445 1900 and 1910 U.S. Census, Lamar County, Alabama).

446 1900 Census, Tallahatchie County, Mississippi); 1920 and 1940 Census (Rosepine, Vernon Parish Louisiana); 1930 Census (Jefferson County, Texas); Louisiana, Find a Grave Index, 1812-2011, *Ancestry.com*.

447 Cecil Harper Jr., "William Lewis Cabell," *The New Handbook of Texas* (Austin, Tx: Texas State Historical Assn., 1996), Vol. 1, 880; Paul Harvey Jr., *Old Tige: General William L. Cabell, C.S.A.* (Hillsboro, Tx: Hill Junior College, 1970), 1-73.

448 1870 and 1880 U.S. Census (Butler County, Alabama); 1900, 1910, and 1920 U.S. Census (Marengo County, Alabama); Vol. Y, p. 492, and Vol. Z, p. 499, Deed Records, Marengo County, Alabama; Marriage Records, Marengo County, Alabama, 1883-1897, p. 314; Alabama, Deaths and Burials Index, 1881-1974, *Ancestry.com*; *Montgomery Advertiser*, as quoted in Hoole, *Rube Burrow*, 141.

449 1860 U.S. Census (Fayette County, Alabama); 1870 U.S. Census (Sanford County, Alabama); 1880 and 1900 U.S. Census (Lamar County, Alabama); Alabama, Marriage Collection, 1800-1969, *Ancestry.com.*; Alabama, Deaths and Burials Index, 1881-1974, *Ancestry.com.*

450 Carruth, *Rube Burrow*, 211; 1880 U.S. Census (Marengo County, Alabama).

451 Miller, *Train Robbing Bunch*, 133-134; 1910 U.S. Census (Madison County, Mississippi); Tennessee, Deaths and Burials Index, 1824-1955, *Ancestry.com*.

452 1880 U.S. Census (Marengo County, Alabama); Carruth, *Rube Burrow*, 213.

453 1880 U.S. Census (Caledonia, Lowndes County, Mississippi).

454 1860, 1870, 1880, and 1900 U.S. Census (Monroe County, Alabama); 1910 U.S. Census (Mobile County, Alabama); *Alabama Deaths and Burials Index, 1881-1974*, Ancestry.Com.

455 Patterson, "Henderson B. Alverson;" "Nancy Adeline Alverson," Ancestry.com.; 1880 U.S. Census (Stephenville, Erath County).

456 "Napoleon Bonapart Thornton," *Ancestry.com*; 1850 U.S. Census (Bienville, Louisiana); 1860 U.S. Census (Stephenville, Erath County, Texas); 1870 U.S. Census (Tarrant County, Texas); 1880 U.S. Census (Erath County, Texas); "Nancy Adeline Alverson Thornton," *Ancestry.Com.*; Vol. J, p. 306; Vol. L, p. 568, and Vol. Q, p. 262, Deed Records, Erath County, Texas; *Stephenville Empire*, 31 March 1883.

Index

Rick Miller

B

myth surrounding, viii, 128–130, 143
nicknames given to, 6, 88
photo of, 3, 4, 82, 121, 122
physical description, 12
researching of, ix–x
on robbery/crime, 28–29
will/estate of, 129, 142–143
young adulthood, 10–13
Burrow, Sarah Francis, 8. See also Cash, Sarah (Burrow)
Burrow, Virginia Catherine (Alverson) "Cata," 5, 10–11, 14, 145, 150, 151
Burrow, William (son of Rube), 88
Burrow, William Jasper, 4
Burrow, William Joseph, 8
Burrow, William Thomas, 11, 148

C

Cabell, Ben E., 22, 26
Cabell, Harriet A. (Rector), 149
Cabell, William Lewis
Askey arrest, 69
background, 148–149
Brock prisoner transfer, 73
communication from, 34
mentioned, 54, 55
photo of, 21
robbery investigations, 26, 27, 33
Cain, W.W., as R. Burrow alias, 74, 88, 179n245
Callahan, J.S., 49, 174n169
Cantrell, G.M., 77
Carney, E.F., 47, 54–55
Carrigan, ___ (officer), 49
Carter, Harvey, 35–36, 37, 52

Carter, Jefferson Davis "Dixie," 103i, 114–117, 124–126, 131, 139–140, 149
Carter, Lenora (McDuffie) "Nora," 149
Carter, Susan, 149
Carter, William, 149
Cash, Eliza Jane, 149
Cash, Henry, 48, 149
Cash, James Alexander
aid/shelter provided by, 66, 72, 98
arrest of, 76, 77, 78
background, 149
communications with, 65, 69
interview with, 88–89
Jewell post office incident, 74–76
mentioned, 56
Cash, Martha Ann. See Burrow, Martha Ann (Cash)
Cash, Sarah (Burrow), 149
Cash, W.H., 88
Cassidy, Butch, viii, 143
Cavin, Thomas, 43
Chattanooga Evening Press, 128
Clark, Ike, 27
Clarke, J.C., 85–86
Clay, John, 90–91
Cleveland, C.B., 126
Cleveland, Osborn, 49
clothes, exhibition of, 130
coffin, of R. Burrow
display of corpse in, 6, 121, 122, 127–128
exhibition of, 130
Cole, John, 27
Conner, Charles, 16, 167n64
Cornett, Brack, 29
Cornett-Whitley gang, 34

Pearre, Charles B., 35, 56, 69, 73
Pendleton robbery, attempted, 35
Pennington, Fillmore (S.F.), 47, 75, 98, 140
Penton, John, 96
photography
of R. Burrow burial plot, 130, 138
of R. Burrow corpse, 121, 122, 127–128
Pinkerton, William, 45
Pinkerton Detective Agency
Genoa investigation, 45–46, 53–54
on R. Burrow, 11
records of, ix
Pittman, __ (man waiting for train), 46
Post Office Department, x, 56, 86, 139–141
Pretty Boy Floyd, vii
Price, H.M., 25, 26, 35
primary sources, vii–viii
Public Enemies (movie), vii
pulp paperback books/potboiler novels, viii, 7

R

railroads. See also specific railroads
corporations as symbol, ix
historical role, 14–15. See also train robberies
Railway Mail Service, 56
Rankin, John, 34
Rathbone, E.G., 140
Ravenscraft, Sam, 27, 37
Reagan, R.B., 34
Rector, Harriet A. See Cabell, Harriet A. (Rector)

"Red Rube! Burrow and His Bloody Career in the Southwest" (Barrett), 88–89
Regional Archives, x
Reno gang, viii–ix, 15
rewards offered
for R. Burrow, 56, 76, 85, 131, 139–141
for train robbers, 78
Roberts, George, 92
Roberts, Drucilla. See Alverson, Drucilla (Roberts)
Ross, L.S. "Sul," 33, 34, 35
Rube Burrow, King of Outlaws (Agee)
about, x, 139
quoted, 8–9, 10, 24, 52, 127

S

Saunders, Kate Wheatley. See Agee, Kate Wheatley (Saunders)
Scholes, Billy, 84
Scott, William, 33
Seay, Thomas, 53, 76, 87, 96, 130–131
secondary sources, viii
Settle, Robert, 27, 37
Shadle, John, 37
Shelton, __ (detective), 94
Shephard, Dick, 17–18
Shield, F.S., 130
Shipp, Ben H., 33, 37
Singleton, __ (man identified by Brock's father-in-law), 46
Singleton, Jack, 149
Sisk, Henry S., 33, 37
Sizer, Robert, 107–109
Skiles, R.T., 32
slickers, as evidence, 44–45